Copyright © 2023 by R. J. Ilyn
All rights reserved. No part of this publication may be used or reproduced in any manner in any medium without prior written permission of the copyright holder.

https://www.BritneyCase.com

Print edition ISBN 979-8-218-30781-3
E-book edition ISBN 979-8-218-30782-0

The Britney Spears Conservatorship Case

Los Angeles Superior Court
Probate Department
Case No. BP 108870

by R. J. Ilyn

Contents

Preface	vii
Prologue	ix
Conservatorship	1
Chapter 1: Involuntary	3
Chapter 2: Capacity	31
Chapter 3: Representation	49
Chapter 4: Come Back	57
Chapter 5: Estate	59
Chapter 6: Compensation	65
Chapter 7: *Britney: For the Record*	81
Chapter 8: Permanent	85
Chapter 9: Mama's Memoir	99
Chapter 10: Defamation	103
Chapter 11: You Better Work	119
Chapter 12: Residency	129
Chapter 13: Break	133
Chapter 14: Dissipate	143
Chapter 15: The Statement	147
Chapter 16: Freed	155
Chapter 17: Accounting	161
Works Cited	167

Preface

Thank you for making time for the result of my years of research. This book is full of excerpts from original court records in Britney Spears's conservatorship case. I aim to add context for the documents and explain some of the regulations of conservatorships.

My hope is that more people will understand conservatorships and guardianships and recognize the need for legal and judicial reform. The Spears case also highlights the need for greater empathy for our fellow humans living with disabilities, no matter their level of wealth or fame.

Prologue

Louisiana's own Britney Jean Spears began performing as a child. Singing in the mirror led to church choir, then local fairs and regional competitions. Training began early with dance lessons and gymnastics classes.

She and her big brother Bryan got through the ups and downs of their parents' marriage together. What began as hometown young love between Jamie and Lynne became years of struggle. Their life together in a small town came with financial strain, drunken arguments, and questions of infidelity.

Little Britney had big talent, a sweet smile, and a drive to perform. Lynne scraped resources together for lessons, costumes, and travels to competitions that always had an entry fee. Eventually mother and daughter made the leap to New York City, hoping for professional success. Performance education and a bit of theatrical and commercial experience in New York paved the way to becoming a Disney girl in Florida.

When Britney was 15, New York lawyer Larry Rudolph began sending out her demo recordings to big city record labels. Jive Records signed the teen and began building her into a solo artist. The professional music industry work began in her 16th year. New chaperone Fe Culotta joined Britney on a working trip to Europe where she created an album with Max Martin. Production rolled into months of radio promotion and mall touring. The first single, *...Baby One More Time,* hit record stores just a few weeks before her 17th birthday in 1998.

The churn of annual albums and tours between 1998 and 2003 left her regularly asking for more downtime and visits with her family. But slowing the churn would slow the revenue and the adults running her career would not allow that.

Britney eventually slowed her career and to focus on her personal life, leading to two marriages and two children. Then personal tragedies and heartaches became a new entertainment churn. Much of the emotional fallout was caught on camera and professionally dissected by journalists. Lesser-known public figures hoping for attention from the cameras joined journalists in scolding the struggling stranger from afar.

Britney continued working through the grief, divorce, and custody battle over her infant children. The 2007 album *Blackout* showcased the innovations given rise by artistic freedom.

Conservatorship

California Superior Court offers this brief description for prospective conservators in probate cases:

What is a conservatorship?

A Conservatorship is a court proceeding in which a judge appoints a family member, friend or other responsible person (conservator) to care for another adult (conservatee) who cannot care for himself/herself and/or his/her finances.

Conservatorship of the Person

When the court appoints you as conservator, you will:
1. Arrange for the conservatee's care and protection;
2. Decide where the conservatee will live; and
3. Are in charge of the following: health care, food, clothes, personal care, housekeeping, transportation, recreation.

Conservatorship of the Estate

When the court appoints you to be the conservator of an estate, you will:
1. Manage the conservatee's finances;
2. Protect the conservatee's income and property;
3. Make a list (inventory) of everything in the estate;
4. Make sure the conservatee's bills are paid;
5. Invest the conservatee's money;

6. Make sure the conservatee gets all the benefits he or she is eligible for;

7. Make sure the conservatee's taxes are filed and paid on time;

8. Keep exact financial records; and

9. Make regular reports of the financial accounts to the court and other interested persons.

(Sup. Ct. of Cal., Cnty of S. Diego, 2019)

Mental Health Conservatorship

In California, there is a separate type of conservatorship to help people who are gravely mentally disabled receive care. These are called LPS Conservatorships, which were established in the Lanterman-Petris-Short Act of 1967. These can be initiated by the patient's treating physician and not by an attorney or family member.

LPS conservatorships are meant to help a person with a serious mental health condition receive care while they recover, for a maximum period of one year. At the end of a year, the conservatee's treating physician can reapply to reestablish the conservatorship.

The process of applying for an LPS Conservatorship begins with a three-day involuntary "5150" hold, followed by a 14-day "5250" hold. At the end of that period, if a physician considers the patient in need of further involuntary detention, a review hearing must be conducted. During that hearing, the patient's level of disability will be certified. The proposed conservatee has the right to request a court hearing or jury trial to determine whether or not they are so gravely mentally disabled that they cannot care for themself or are a danger to themself or others. (Cal. Cts., n.d.)

Chapter 1

Involuntary

In December 2007, Jamie Spears began working to bring his daughter Britney Spears back under his control with the help of Louise "Lou" Taylor. Ms. Taylor had already been working as the business manager of his youngest daughter, Jamie Lynn Spears. In early January 2008, a dispute over where Britney's babies would stay for the night turned into Los Angeles Police Department officers at the door. EMTs strapped the young mother into an ambulance to University of California, Los Angeles Cedars-Sinai Medical Center in Westwood.

California law gave everyone the right to call and request a 5150 involuntary psychiatric hold on anyone else. These emergency holds could last for a maximum of three days. The day after Britney's late-night admission, doctors determined that she was not a threat to herself or others and discharged her a day early.

The powerfully famous and wealthy young woman became more and more vulnerable. Jamie responded to his daughter's struggles with a push to take charge.

According to mom Lynne Spears, Jamie and Ms. Taylor planned to file for a conservatorship over Britney on January 22, 2008. (Craker & Spears, 2008) Lawyers specializing in conserving people, particularly wealthy ones, were on the job. Jeryl Cohen, Vivian Thoreen, and Geraldine Wyle of Luce, Forward, Hamilton & Scripps were ready to file Jamie's petition to Los Angeles Superior Court's Probate Department. But the paperwork would not be enough to conserve Britney if she mounted a legal fight. Her child custody dispute with ex-husband Kevin Federline gave them an opportunity to file their conservatorship applications while she was indisposed.

Britney had developed a public reputation of being mentally unstable and abusing drugs. Her family law attorneys at the firm of Trope & Trope made a plan to combat that reputation. Friend Sam Lutfi recounted his experiences in January 2008 in a declaration in his defamation case against the Spears'.[1] Mr. Lutfi recalled,

> At some point, Britney's family law attorneys retained a psychiatrist, Deborah Nadel, M.D., who began making nightly house calls. Dr. Nadel cautioned me that Britney would either have to take her medication or she was going to order a second WIC § 5150 hold. I was unable to get Britney to take her medication and Dr. Nadel ordered the second 5150 'hold' on January 31, 2008.

Around 1 a.m. on Thursday, January 31, a team of L.A.P.D. officers and Los Angeles Fire Department crew stormed Britney's home and repeated the 5150 process. According to an L.A.P.D. representative speaking to *The Los Angeles Times* later that morning, barriers along the street in front of her house had already been erected and the airspace above the gated community was cleared to keep cameras and the journalists holding them from interfering. A caravan of officers in cars, on motorcycles, and in helicopters escorted the ambulance from Britney's Beverly Hills home to U.C.L.A. Medical Center, where Dr. Nadel worked, at a reported cost of $25,000 in taxpayer

---

[1] Sam Lutfi vs. Lynne Irene Spears, et al. LASC Case BC 406904. (*See* Chapter 10: Defamation)

funds. (Blankstein, Gold, & Winton, 2008) By 5:00 am local time on February 1, *People* magazine already had "sources" sharing that Dr. Nadel "had instigated Spears's second hospitalization". (McGee, 2008)

On January 31, Jamie and his attorneys signed the applications for the conservatorships of Britney's estate and person. The next morning, Friday, February 1, Jamie and his team filed their petition for conservatorship at Stanley Mosk Courthouse in advance of a 10:30 a.m. hearing. According to family friend Jacqueline Butcher, Judge Reva Goetz approved the petition within ten minutes, an all too common timeframe for probate conservatorships. (Farrow & Tolentino, 2021)

Britney's loss of rights began when Judge Aviva Bobb ordered the appointment of Samuel Ingham as her attorney two days before he met Britney, and without a medical professional's report on her mental state:

ORDER APPOINTING COUNSEL

The Court on its own motion appoints SAMUEL D. INGHAM to act as counsel for BRITNEY SPEARS, the proposed conservatee.

Pursuant to Civil Code Section 56.10(b) (1) and HIPAA Regulation 45CFR Section 164.512(e) (1) (i) the Court orders that counsel appointed herein shall have access to and authority to review and copy the medical records of BRITNEY SPEARS, the proposed conservatee, without her consent.

Date: February 1, 2008

Mr. Ingham already had years of experience in conserving wealthy Californians. On Sunday, February 3, he spoke with Britney at the hospital for 15 minutes. In his professional legal opinion, she lacked the mental capacity to hire a lawyer. Mr. Ingham kindly volunteered to take on that role for which he would eventually be paid $10,000 per week.

Jamie took charge of Britney's person and estate by applying for a pair of probate conservatorships:

> Do NOT use this form for a temporary conservatorship.
>
> Form GC-310 (Rev. January 1, 2006)
>
> Filed by Geraldine Wyle, Jeryll Cohan, [sic] and Vivian Thoreen of Luce, Forward, Hamilton & Scripps LLP
>
> with Los Angeles Superior Court February 1, 2008 fees paid $799.00
>
> ### CONSERVATORSHIP OF Britney Jean Spears proposed CONSERVATEE
>
> ### PETITION FOR APPOINTMENT OF PROBATE CONSERVATOR OF THE PERSON CASE NUMBER: BP108870
>
> 1. Petitioner James P. Spears requests that [self]
> a. be appointed conservator of the ESTATE of the proposed conservatee and Letters issue upon qualification.
> b. James P. Spears be appointed conservator of the PERSON of the proposed conservatee and Letters issue upon qualification.
> c. (2) bond be fixed at: $
> d. orders authorizing independent exercise of powers under Probate Code section 2590[i] be granted. Granting the proposed conservator of the estate powers to be exercised independently under Probate Code section 2590[ii] would be to the advantage and benefit and in the

best interest of the conservatorship estate.

g. the proposed conservatee be adjudged to lack the capacity to give informed consent for the medical treatment or healing by prayer and that the proposed conservator of the person be granted the powers specified in Probate Code section 2355[iii]

k. orders related to dementia placement or treatment as specified in the *Attachment Requesting Special Orders Regarding Dementia* (form GC-313) under Probate Code section 2356.5[iv] be granted. A *Capacity Declaration—Conservatorship* (form GC-335) and *Dementia Attachment to Capacity Declaration—Conservatorship* (form GC-335A), executed by a licensed physician or by a licensed psychologist acting within the scope of his or her licensure with at least two years experience diagnosing dementia will be filed before the hearing.

L. other orders be granted (Specify in Attachment 11.)

2. **Proposed conservatee** *is* Britney Jean Spears *(Present address):* UCLA Medical Center, 10833 Le Conte Avenue, Westwood, California 90095

3. a. **Jurisdictional facts** *(initial appointment only):*
The proposed conservatee has no conservator in California and is a resident of California and a resident of this county.

b. **Petitioner**
(1) is not a **creditor** or an agent of a creditor of the proposed conservatee.
(2) is not a **debtor** or an agent of a debtor of the pro-

posed conservatee.

c. **Proposed conservator** is (4) a relative of the proposed conservatee as *(specify relationship):* father

c. Character and estimated value of the property of the estate Unknown

5. a. **Proposed conservatee** (initial appointment of conservator only) is an adult.

5. c. **Proposed conservatee** requires a conservator and is (1) unable to properly provide for his or her personal needs for physical health, food, clothing, or shelter. Supporting fact are as follows:
See Confidential Supplemental Information.

5. e. Confidential Supplemental Information (form GC-312) is filed with this petition. (Initial appointment of conservator only. All petitioners must file this form except banks and other entities authorized to do business as a trust company.)

8. **Proposed conservatee is not the petitioner AND has not nominated the proposed conservator.** [emphasis added]

9. Medical treatment of proposed conservatee
a. There is no form of medical treatment for which the proposed conservatee has the capacity to give an informed consent.
b. A *Capacity Declaration—Conservatorship* (form GC-335) executed by a licensed physician or by a licensed psychologist acting within the scope of his or her

licensure, stating the proposed conservatee lacks the capacity to give informed consent for any form of medical treatment and giving reasons and the factual basis for this conclusion, will be filed before the hearing.

10. Temporary conservatorship

Filed with this petition is a Petition for Appointment of Temporary Guardian or Conservator (form GC-110).

California Probate Code gave a conservator of the person powers over the conservatee and their finances, but conservatees maintained some key rights.

THE CONSERVATEE'S RIGHTS

Conservatees do not lose all rights or all voice in important decisions affecting their lives. All conservatees have the right to be treated with understanding and respect, the right to have their wishes considered, and the right to be well cared for by their conservators. Conservatees generally keep the right to (1) control their own wages or salary from employment, (2) make or change a will, (3) marry, (4) receive personal mail, (5) be represented by a lawyer, (6) ask a judge to change conservators, (7) ask a judge to end the conservatorship, (8) vote, unless a judge decides they are not capable of exercising this right, (9) control personal spending money if a judge has authorized an allowance, and (10) make their own medical decisions, unless a judge has taken away that right and given it exclusively to their conservators. (Sup. Ct. of Cal., Cnty of S. Diego, 2019)

Jamie did not stop at typical conservator powers. In the petition he signed on January 31, he asked Judge Goetz for more, including the power to ask hospital staff to use restraints on his daughter:

> Attachment 1.d Petitioner requests that the Court grant the Conservator of the Person the following powers in addition to the powers provided by law:
>
> 1. ~~The power to make all medical and health care decisions for the Conservatee under Probate Code Section 2355, including but not limited to, the power to consent to and authorize hospitalization and a full medical evaluation and diagnostic tests, including but not limited to, blood work-up, urine test, psychiatric evaluation, to prevent the Conservatee from discharging herself from the hospital, to authorize the hospital to use security personnel to prevent the conservatee from leaving the hospital and to authorize the medical staff to use restraints, if necessary, and recommended by the Conservatee's treating physician.~~ *[Request denied by Judge Goetz]*
>
> 2. The power to restrict and limit visitors; provided that the Temporary Conservator shall not prevent the Conservatee from meeting with her attorney, subject to the Temporary Conservator's approval of the location for the meeting and ability to secure it in order to protect the Conservatee.
>
> 3. The power to retain caretakers for the Conservatee on a 24 hour/7 day basis. The power to retain security guards for the Conservatee on a 24 hour/7 day basis.

Judge Goetz did not approve the first request about controlling Britney's medical and health care decisions, but did add, "The power to prosecute civil harassment restraining orders that the temporary conservator deems appropriate." Jamie immediately used that power to file for restraining orders on Britney's friends Sam Lutfi and Adnan Ghalib.

The application for appointment of an estate conservator added another attorney, Andrew Wallet. Mr. Wallet had professional experience with managing estates and joined Jamie as co-conservator of the estate only:

> Do NOT use this form for a temporary conservatorship.
>
> Filed by Geraldine Wyle, Jeryll Cohan, [sic] and Vivian Thoreen of Luce, Forward, Hamilton & Scripps LLP
>
> with Los Angeles Superior Court February 1, 2008
>
> CONSERVATORSHIP OF Britney Jean Spears
> PROPOSED CONSERVATEE
>
> PETITION FOR APPOINTMENT OF PROBATE
> CONSERVATOR OF THE ESTATE
> CASE NUMBER: BP108870

1. Petitioner James P. Spears requests that James P. Spears and Andrew M. Wallet
a. be appointed conservator of the ESTATE of the proposed conservatee and Letters issue upon qualification.
c. (2) bond be fixed at: $
d. orders authorizing independent exercise of powers under Probate Code section 2590 be granted. Granting the proposed conservator of the estate powers to be exercised independently under Probate Code section

2590 would be to the advantage and benefit and in the best interest of the conservatorship estate.
(Specify orders, powers, and reasons in Attachment 1d.)
g. the proposed conservatee be adjudged to lack the capacity to give informed consent for the medical treatment or healing by prayer and that the proposed conservator of the person be granted the powers specified in Probate Code section 2355 *(Complete item 9 on page 5.)*
k. orders related to dementia placement or treatment as specified in the *Attachment Requesting Special Orders Regarding Dementia* (form GC-313) under Probate Code section 2356.5 be granted. A *Capacity Declaration — Conservatorship* (form GC-335) and *Dementia Attachment to Capacity Declaration — Conservatorship* (form GC-335A), executed by a licensed physician or by a licensed psychologist acting within the scope of his or her licensure with at least two years experience diagnosing dementia will be filed before the hearing.

L. other orders be granted (Specify in Attachment 1l.)

2. **Proposed conservatee** *is* Britney Jean Spears
(Present address): UCLA Medical Center,
10833 Le Conte Avenue, Westwood, California 90095

3. a. **Jurisdictional facts** *(initial appointment only):*
The proposed conservatee has no conservator in California and is a resident of California and a resident of this county.

b. Petitioner
(1) is not a **creditor** or an agent of a creditor of the pro-

posed conservatee.

(2) is not a **debtor** or an agent of a debtor of the proposed conservatee.

c. Proposed conservator is (4) a relative of the proposed conservatee as *(specify relationship):* father
(7) a private professional conservator, as defined in Probate Code section 2341, who has filed with the court the information statement required by Probate Code section 2342. (Andrew M. Wallet)
(8) registered with the Statewide Registry of Private Conservators, Guardians, and Trustees maintained by the California Department of Justice under Probate Code sections 2850-2855.

d. **Petitioner** is (4) a relative of the proposed conservatee as *(specify relationship):* father (James P. Spears)
(8) the proposed conservator. (Andrew M. Wallet)

e. Character and estimated value of the property of the estate Unknown

4. a. **Proposed conservatee** (initial appointment of conservator only) is an adult.

5. c. **Proposed conservatee** requires a conservator and is (2) substantially unable to manage his or her financial resources or to resist fraud or undue influence. Supporting facts are as follows:
See Confidential Supplemental Information.

5. e. Confidential Supplemental Information (form GC-312) is filed with this petition. (Initial appointment of

conservator only. All petitioners must file this form except banks and other entities authorized to do business as a trust company.)

8. **Proposed conservatee <u>is not the petitioner AND has not nominated the proposed conservator.</u>** [emphasis added]

9. **Medical treatment of proposed conservatee**
b. A *Capacity Declaration—Conservatorship* (form GC-335) executed by a licensed physician or by a licensed psychologist acting within the scope of his or her licensure stating that the proposed conservatee lacks the capacity to give informed consent for any form of medical treatment and giving reasons and the factual basis for this conclusion, will be filed before the hearing.

10. **Temporary conservatorship**
Filed with this petition is a *Petition for Appointment of Temporary Guardian or Conservator* (form GC-110).

Similar to Jamie's additional powers in the application for a conservatorship of the person, he and Mr. Wallet requested additional estate conservator powers. However, Judge Goetz did not approve all of their requests:

> Attachment 1.d The Petitioner Requests that the Court grant the Conservator of the Estate the following powers in addition to powers provided by law:
>
> 1. ~~The power to obtain all documents and records relating to the Conservatee and her assets, whether held in her name or in the name of another, including but not~~

~~limited to, all records currently in the possession and control of the Conservatee's business manager, Howard Grossman, her attorneys, and other, all contracts, information relating to credit cards, bank statements, estate planning documents, and receivables.~~ *[Request denied by Judge Goetz]*

2. The power to take all actions necessary to secure the Conservatee's assets, including the power to enter and take possession and control of the Conservatee's residence, identified in the Confidential Supplemental Information, to remove all persons from the residence and take any and all actions necessary to secure the residence, including changing the locks, call on law enforcement and employ security guards at the expense of the Conservatorship Estate.

3. The power to take all actions necessary to secure the Conservatee's liquid assets, including but not limited to, the power to cancel all credit cards.

4. The power to revoke all powers of attorneys, including powers of attorney for making health care decisions and managing real estate, and to terminate any and all agencies.

5. The power to commence and maintain litigation and participate in any litigation with respect to which the Conservatee is a part or has an interest, and the power to retain counsel and experts, and to pay same from the Conservatorship Estate.
[Judge Goetz note: "related to the Family Law case."]

6. Pursuant to Probate Code Section 2590 the following powers set forth in Probate Code Section 2591:

a. To contract for the conservatorship and perform outstanding contracts and thereby bind the estate. *[Judge Goetz note: "including confidentiality agreements"]*

b. ~~To operate at the risk of the estate a business constituting an asset of the estate.~~ *[Request denied by Judge Goetz]*

c. ~~To pay, collect, compromise, arbitrate, or otherwise adjust claims, debts, or demands upon the Conservatorship Estate.~~ *[Request denied by Judge Goetz]*

d. ~~To employ attorneys, accountants, investment counsel, agents, depositaries, and employees and to pay the expenses, and the power to fire any of the same.~~ *[Request denied by Judge Goetz]*

7. The Conservatee is to remain in California pending the hearing on the Petition for Appointment of Permanent Conservator, the written consent of the Conservator of the Person, or further order of the Court.

[Judge Goetz note: 8. Temporary conservators have the power to prosecute Civil Harassment Restraining orders that they deem to be appropriate.]

The final blow to Britney's freedom was Judge Goetz approving a request for an exception to a key California statute.

According to California Probate Code § 2250, a proposed conservator was legally required to notify the proposed conservatee five days in advance of the conservatorship hearing. Judicial Council of California explained,

A copy of *Notice of Hearing—Guardianship or Conserva-*

torship ("Notice") must be "served" on—delivered to—each person who has the right under law to be notified of the date, time, place, and purpose of a court hearing in a guardianship or conservatorship. Copies of this Notice may be served by mail in most situations. The petitioner (the person who requested the court hearing) **may not personally perform either service by mail or personal service**, but must show the court that copies of this Notice have been served in a way the law allows. The petitioner does this by arranging for someone else to perform the service and complete and sign a proof of service, which the petitioner then files with the original Notice. [emphasis supplied]
(Sup. Ct. of Cal., Cnty of S. Diego, 2019)

The five-days notice of a petition to conserve someone gave the proposed conservatee time to respond to the petition. They were even entitled to a jury trial to decide their fate.

Ms. Wyle successfully argued on February 1 that giving Britney the standard five-days notice would interfere with their conservatorship petition. If she knew what was happening to her she might tell someone, such as Mr. Lutfi:

EX PARTE APPLICATION FOR ORDER FINDING GOOD CAUSE FOR EXCUSING NOTICE OF HEARING ON PETITION FOR APPOINTMENT OF TEMPORARY CONSERVATOR OF THE PERSON; MEMORANDUM OF POINTS AND AUTHORITIES

Pursuant to Cal. Prob. Code § 2250 and Cal. R. Court 7.1062, applicant James P. Spears ("Applicant"), the father of the proposed conservatee Britney Jean Spears

("Britney"), will, and hereby does, respectfully apply to the Court for an Order finding that there is good cause for not giving notice of the hearing on the proposed appointment of a temporary conservator and, in the alternative, for waiving the requirement that notice be given five days before the hearing. Good cause exists for waiving the notice requirement because: (1) Britney or her estate may suffer immediate and substantial harm if Applicant is required to give five days' notice before the hearing, *see* Cal. R. Court 7.1062(d)(1); (2) Britney's medical treatment may be impaired if she is given notice prior to the hearing, *see* Cal. R. Court 7.1062(d)(2); (3) giving notice of the hearing would give notice to Osama ("Sam") Lutfi of the hearing, and there is a substantial risk that he might cause harm to Britney or her estate in advance of the hearing, *see id.;* and (4) there is an immediate and substantial medical emergency justifying waiver of the notice requirement, *see* Cal. R. Court 7.1062(d)(3), because Britney was on the morning of January 31, 2008 placed on a 72-hour hold pursuant to Cal. Welf. & Inst. Code § 5150 that expires on Sunday, February 3, 2008, less than five days after the date on which this *ex parte* application will be heard.

This application is based on this Application, the Memorandum of Points and Authorities filed concurrently herewith, the Declarations of Lynne Spears, James P. Spears, and Geraldine A. Wyle filed concurrently herewith, the [Proposed] Order lodged concurrently herewith, and such argument as may be presented in connection with the Application.

As set forth in the Declaration of Geraldine A. Wyle filed concurrently herewith, Applicant has not given notice to Britney of this Application. This *ex parte* application asks the Court to find that there is good cause for not giving notice of the hearing on the proposed appointment of a temporary conservator. Giving notice of the *ex parte* application would give Britney notice of the hearing on the proposed appointment of a temporary conservatory, contrary to the relief sought by this application.

Wyle's application included supporting statements from Britney's parents. First, proposed conservatee dad Jamie:

Early on the morning of January 31, 2008, Britney was admitted to UCLA Medical Center on a 5150, a 72-hour psychiatric hold.

On January 31, 2008, despite instructions given by my wife Lynne Spears and me, Osama ("Sam") Lutfi was allowed to visit Britney at the hospital.

Based upon my observation of Britney's emotional and psychological condition and her dealings with Mr. Lutfi, I believe that Britney is incapable of keeping information from Mr. Lutfi. In particular, I believe that, if she knew that I was planning to seek a conservatorship for her, she would tell Mr. Lutfi about the planned conservatorship.

However, Jamie did informally tell her about the conservatorship while she was in the hospital over the weekend, as he stated in his February 4, 2008 declaration.

Lynne also contributed to the application to waive notice:

> This past Monday night (January 28), Britney's father, Jamie, and I (in separate cars) went to Britney's house in Beverly Hills because we had heard news reports that Britney had just been in a big fight with Osama Lufti [sic] aka Sam Lufti ("Sam"), the man who has inserted himself into my daughter's life, home, and finances, and that she was crying. We were very concerned about her safety. We arrived at the Summit Community gatehouse in BHPO at approximately 10 p.m. I was with my friend, Jackie [Butcher].
>
> The guards at the gatehouse stopped us there for awhile. Jackie, Jamie, and I finally proceeded to Britney's house and entered it. We were able to enter the house because it was not locked. Britney does not lock her doors and currently there are no security guards around her residence. Britney was not home. We found Sam, and Sam said as we walked in the door that Britney only wanted me to come to the house, and that she was afraid to see her dad.
>
> Two or three paparazzi came into the house and entered the kitchen. They greeted Sam. The paparazzi then reported to Sam where Britney currently was. From the conversation between Sam and the paparazzi I determined that Sam had given Felipe (another paparazzi) one of Britney's cars to get her out of the house when he heard that Jamie and I were on our way to see Britney. I also understood from the conversation that Sam dis-

abled all of Britney's cars (she has several at her residence).

Sam had told Britney that Jamie and I were coming to the house to do an intervention, and that Britney panicked and took off with Felipe.

Lynne's declaration also included accusations of alcohol and prescription drug abuse by Britney. She accused Mr. Lutfi of making threats to herself and abusing Britney. This narrative was the basis for the February 1 restraining order application against Messrs. Lutfi and Ghalib. It was also included in an application to seal records of the conservatorship of the person rather than redacting specific instances of private information. In her memoir, *Through the Storm,* Lynne and co-author Lorilee Craker expanded on and refined her account of January 28. (Craker & Spears, 2008)[2]

Documents filed in a court in the United States are in the public record. They are available for the general public to view, allowing for judicial oversight. Some documents made public include redactions to protect specific sensitive information of people involved in the case, such as financial details and contact information.

Exceptions to public access to court documents are made for particularly sensitive information. This can include details about medical conditions and minor children. A party to the case can petition a judge to seal these public records from the general public. Ms. Cohen's application to seal records of Britney's case focused on medical privacy:

Pursuant to Cal. R. Court 2.550 and 2.551, applicant

---

[2] *See* Chapter 9: Mama's Memoir

> James P. Spears ("Applicant") will, and hereby does, respectfully apply to the Court for an Order sealing the record of these proceedings. Applicant seeks such relief in connection with his petition for the appointment of a conservator over the person of his daughter, Britney Jean Spears ("Britney"). Applicant requests that these proceedings be sealed to protect Britney's constitutionally protected privacy rights as well as her prospects for a medical recovery.
>
> This application is made on the grounds that a sealing order is required under Cal. R. Court 2.550(d) because the facts establish:
>
> (1) There exists an overriding interest that overcomes the right of public access to the record;
> (2) The overriding interest supports sealing the record;
> (3) A substantial probability exists that the overriding interest will be prejudiced if the record is not sealed;
> (4) The proposed sealing is narrowly tailored; and
> (5) No less restrictive means exist to achieve the overriding interest.

Although Jamie requested that all of the conservatorship records be completely sealed, on February 4, 2008, Judge Goetz ordered that only HIPAA-protected medical information in the conservatorship of the person be sealed.

The records that were publicly available detailed liberties lost, including the constitutional right to a choice of lawyer, a jury trial, and freedom of movement. Britney was legally no longer her own person. According to the court-ordered probate conservatorship, Jamie was the only person who had the legal right to act as Britney Spears.

In a private room at U.C.L.A. Medical Center, Britney tried to figure out who was responsible for her situation and who could end it. Mr. Lutfi sat by her side while her parents were barred from the room. When he was out on a burger run, Lynne gave the treating physician her account of Mr. Lutfi abusing Britney. The physician decided to bar any visitors from Britney's room until the situation stabilized. (Craker & Spears, 2008)

During the first weekend of the conservatorship, Jamie came and went from U.C.L.A. Medical Center, facing questions from Britney in person and on the phone. He could not stay by her side. The third day of her hospital stay was Super Bowl Sunday and he was responsible for catering a watch party. A houseful of NFL fans needed his BBQ. Britney interrupted his work with repeated demanding calls.

He recalled the weekend in his declaration to the Court on February 4, 2008:

> On Saturday, February 2, 2008, I spent approximately 8 hours at UCLA, where Britney is hospitalized, meeting with Britney's treating physician and visiting with Britney, together with Britney's mother, Lynne Spears.
>
> On Sunday, February 3, 2008, I was unable to visit the hospital during he day because I had to work; I am a cook, and I was catering a large Super Bowl party.
>
> While I was working, Britney called me on my cell phone at least four (4) times. She called me about every twenty (20) minutes.
>
> Britney first called me at approximately 1:30 p.m. She said, "Daddy, what are you doing?" I told her that I was cooking. Britney said, "What are you doing cooking,

Daddy, why are you not here with me?" I told her, "Baby, Daddy's got to work." She asked me, "How long are you working?" I told her for a few hours. I then told her, "Daddy has to get back to work.

About twenty minutes later, Britney called me again. She said, "How long are you going to be, Daddy?" I told her that I didn't know. She said, "Hurry up and get here." I asked her why. She said, "Because you got to get me out of here." I told her that I could not get her out of there. She said, "I want you to." I asked her whether she wanted me to bring her anything, and she said, "Yes, bring me some ice cream." I asked her what flavor. She said, "Vanilla."

She called me a third time, about twenty minutes after the second call. She asked me again, "When are you going to be here, Daddy?" I told her I was working, but that I would be there as soon as I could.

At approximately 2:30 p.m. Lynne called me from the hospital and told me that Britney wanted to talk to me. Lynne put Britney on the phone. Britney asked again when I was going to get to the hospital to see her.

I told her I would be there as soon as I got cleaned up, after everyone began eating and after I could make sure that my staff would be able to clean everything up. I told her that I would be at the hospital before 5:00 p.m. She said, "Hurry up, Daddy."

When I arrived at the hospital, Britney was lying down. I leaned over to kiss her. She turned her head away from me. I said to her, "I love you." Britney said, "No, you don't."

Britney then got up and said to me, "The doctor told me that you are keeping me in here." I said, "No, I'm not keeping you in here." Britney said, "Someone's lying. You put me in here."

One of the hospital nurses brought Britney the Doctor's orders so Britney could see them. Britney wouldn't look at them. The nurse said to Britney, "Ms. Spears, your daddy did not put you in here. Your daddy is not keeping you in here. The hospital is keeping you in here."

Britney then said to me, "Come on, Daddy. Let's get out of here. Talk [sic] my hand and let's walk out of here together." I then said to her, "I wish I could, but I can't."

Britney was getting agitated.

We then started to talk about Britney's children. I said to her, "Do you want me to help you get your babies back?" I asked her if she wanted me to help her with her kids.

Britney told me that she had fired her lawyers and that she has new lawyers.

I told her that she doesn't have new lawyers with the kids. She told me, "No, I have new lawyers that will help me with my stuff."

I told her that she has two sets of lawyers. Britney said "No. I have fired those lawyers." I told her that she had a new lawyer in the conservatorship, but not the child stuff. I asked her if she wanted me to help her with her children, that I would help her.

Britney then told me that there was some property of hers that Sam Lutfi had wrongfully taken. She asked me to help her get it back. I told her that I would.

Britney also called for professional legal help. Probate attorney Adam Streisand agreed to represent her in the conservatorship case and began reaching out to Jamie's attorneys, Mses. Wyle and Thoreen.

On Sunday, February 3, the three-day limit of the 5150 involuntary psychiatric hold on Britney rolled into a 5250 14-day hold. Although anyone could request a 5150 hold on anyone else in California, only medical professionals could force a 5250 involuntary hold if the patient was not deemed mentally well enough to leave the facility after three days.

California Probate Code

[i]Section 2590. (Amended by Stats. 2007, Ch. 553, Sec. 18.)
(a)The court may, in its discretion, make an order granting the guardian or conservator any one or more or all of the powers specified in Section 2591 if the court determines that, under the circumstances of the particular guardianship or conservatorship, it would be to the advantage, benefit, and best interest of the estate to do so. Subject only to the requirements, conditions, or limitations as are specifically and expressly provided, either directly or by reference, in the order granting the power or powers, and if consistent with Section 2591, the guardian or conservator may exercise the granted power or powers without notice, hearing, or court authorization, instructions, approval, or confirmation in the same manner as the ward or conservatee could do if possessed of legal capacity.
(b)The guardian or conservator does not have a power specified in Section 2591 without authorization by a court under this article or other express provisions of this code.

[ii]Section 2591. (Amended by Stats. 2007, Ch. 553, Sec. 19.)
The powers referred to in Section 2590 are:
(a)The power to operate, for a period longer than 45 days, at the risk of the estate a business, farm, or enterprise constituting an asset of the estate.
(b)The power to grant and take options.

(c)(1)The power to sell at public or private sale real or personal property of the estate without confirmation of the court of the sale, other than the personal residence of a conservatee.
(2)The power to sell at public or private sale the personal residence of the conservatee as described in Section 2591.5 without confirmation of the court of the sale. The power granted pursuant to this paragraph is subject to the requirements of Sections 2352.5 and 2541.
(3)For purposes of this subdivision, authority to sell property includes authority to contract for the sale and fulfill the terms and conditions of the contract, including conveyance of the property.
(d)The power to create by grant or otherwise easements and servitudes.
(e)The power to borrow money.
(f)The power to give security for the repayment of a loan.
(g)The power to purchase real or personal property.
(h)The power to alter, improve, raze, replace, and rebuild property of the estate.
(i)The power to let or lease property of the estate, or extend, renew, or modify a lease of real property, for which the monthly rental or lease term exceeds the maximum specified in Sections 2501 and 2555 for any purpose (including exploration for and removal of gas, oil, and other minerals and natural resources) and for any period, including a term commencing at a future time.
(j)The power to lend money on adequate security.
(k)The power to exchange property of the estate.
(l)The power to sell property of the estate on credit if any unpaid portion of the selling price is adequately secured.
(m)The power to commence and maintain an action for partition.
(n)The power to exercise stock rights and stock options.
(o)The power to participate in and become subject to and to consent to the provisions of a voting trust and of a reorganization, consolidation, merger, dissolution, liquidation, or other modification or adjustment affecting estate property.
(p)The power to pay, collect, compromise, or otherwise adjust claims, debts, or demands upon the guardianship or conservatorship described in subdivision (a) of Section 2501, Section 2502 or 2504, or to arbitrate any dispute described in Section 2406.

[iii]Section 2355. (Amended by Stats. 1999, Ch. 658, Sec. 12.)
(a) If the conservatee has been adjudicated to lack the capacity to make health care decisions, the conservator has the exclusive authority to make health care decisions for the conservatee that the conservator in good faith based on medical advice determines to be necessary. The conservator shall make health care decisions for the conservatee in accordance with the conservatee's individual health care instructions, if any, and other wishes to the extent known to the conservator. Otherwise, the conservator shall make the decision in accordance with the conservator's determination of the conservatee's best interest. In determining the conservatee's best interest, the

conservator shall consider the conservatee's personal values to the extent known to the conservator. The conservator may require the conservatee to receive the health care, whether or not the conservatee objects. In this case, the health care decision of the conservator alone is sufficient and no person is liable because the health care is administered to the conservatee without the conservatee's consent.

[vi]Section 2356.5. (Amended by Stats. 2003, Ch. 32, Sec. 2.)
(a)The Legislature hereby finds and declares:
(1)That people with dementia, as defined in the last published edition of the "Diagnostic and Statistical Manual of Mental Disorders," should have a conservatorship to serve their unique and special needs.
(2)That, by adding powers to the probate conservatorship for people with dementia, their unique and special needs can be met. This will reduce costs to the conservatee and the family of the conservatee, reduce costly administration by state and county government, and safeguard the basic dignity and rights of the conservatee.
(3)That it is the intent of the Legislature to recognize that the administration of psychotropic medications has been, and can be, abused by care-givers and, therefore, granting powers to a conservator to authorize these medications for the treatment of dementia requires the protections specified in this section.
(b)Notwithstanding any other provision of law, a conservator may authorize the placement of a conservatee in a secured perimeter residential care facility for the elderly operated pursuant to Section 1569.698 of the Health and Safety Code, or a locked and secured nursing facility which specializes in the care and treatment of people with dementia pursuant to subdivision (c) of Section 1569.691 of the Health and Safety Code, and which has a care plan that meets the requirements of Section 87724 of Title 22 of the California Code of Regulations, upon a court's finding, by clear and convincing evidence, of all of the following:
(1)The conservatee has dementia, as defined in the last published edition of the "Diagnostic and Statistical Manual of Mental Disorders."
(2)The conservatee lacks the capacity to give informed consent to this placement and has at least one mental function deficit pursuant to subdivision (a) of Section 811, and this deficit significantly impairs the person's ability to understand and appreciate the consequences of his or her actions pursuant to subdivision (b) of Section 811.
(3)The conservatee needs or would benefit from a restricted and secure environment, as demonstrated by evidence presented by the physician or psychologist referred to in paragraph (3) of subdivision (f).
(4)The court finds that the proposed placement in a locked facility is the least restrictive placement appropriate to the needs of the conservatee.
(c)Notwithstanding any other provision of law, a conservator of a person may authorize the administration of medications appropriate for the care and treatment of dementia, upon a court's finding, by clear and convincing evidence, of all of the following:

(1)The conservatee has dementia, as defined in the last published edition of the "Diagnostic and Statistical Manual of Mental Disorders."
(2)The conservatee lacks the capacity to give informed consent to the administration of medications appropriate to the care of dementia, and has at least one mental function deficit pursuant to subdivision (a) of Section 811, and this deficit or deficits significantly impairs the person's ability to understand and appreciate the consequences of his or her actions pursuant to subdivision (b) of Section 811.
(3)The conservatee needs or would benefit from appropriate medication as demonstrated by evidence presented by the physician or psychologist referred to in paragraph (3) of subdivision (f).
(d)Pursuant to subdivision (b) of Section 2355, in the case of a person who is an adherent of a religion whose tenets and practices call for a reliance on prayer alone for healing, the treatment required by the conservator under subdivision (c) shall be by an accredited practitioner of that religion in lieu of the administration of medications.
(e)A conservatee who is to be placed in a facility pursuant to this section shall not be placed in a mental health rehabilitation center as described in Section 5675 of the Welfare and Institutions Code, or in an institution for mental disease as described in Section 5900 of the Welfare and Institutions Code.
(f)A petition for authority to act under this section shall be governed by Section 2357, except:
(1)The conservatee shall be represented by an attorney pursuant to Chapter 4 (commencing with Section 1470) of Part 1.
(2)The conservatee shall be produced at the hearing, unless excused pursuant to Section 1893.
(3)The petition shall be supported by a declaration of a licensed physician, or a licensed psychologist within the scope of his or her licensure, regarding each of the findings required to be made under this section for any power requested, except that the psychologist has at least two years of experience in diagnosing dementia.
(4)The petition may be filed by any of the persons designated in Section 1891.
(g)The court investigator shall annually investigate and report to the court every two years pursuant to Sections 1850 and 1851 if the conservator is authorized to act under this section. In addition to the other matters provided in Section 1851, the conservatee shall be specifically advised by the investigator that the conservatee has the right to object to the conservator's powers granted under this section, and the report shall also include whether powers granted under this section are warranted. If the conservatee objects to the conservator's powers granted under this section, or the investigator determines that some change in the powers granted under this section is warranted, the court shall provide a copy of the report to the attorney of record for the conservatee. If no attorney has been appointed for the conservatee, one shall be appointed pursuant to Chapter 4 (commencing with Section 1470) of Part 1. The attorney shall, within 30 days after receiving

this report, do one of the following:
(1) File a petition with the court regarding the status of the conservatee.
(2) File a written report with the court stating that the attorney has met with the conservatee and determined that the petition would be inappropriate.
(h) A petition to terminate authority granted under this section shall be governed by Section 2359.
(i) Nothing in this section shall be construed to affect a conservatorship of the estate of a person who has dementia.
(j) Nothing in this section shall affect the laws that would otherwise apply in emergency situations.
(k) Nothing in this section shall affect current law regarding the power of a probate court to fix the residence of a conservatee or to authorize medical treatment for any conservatee who has not been determined to have dementia.
(l)(1) Until such time as the conservatorship becomes subject to review pursuant to Section 1850, this section shall not apply to a conservatorship established on or before the effective date of the adoption of Judicial Council forms that reflect the procedures authorized by this section, or January 1, 1998, whichever occurs first.
(2) Upon the adoption of Judicial Council forms that reflect the procedures authorized by this section or January 1, 1998, whichever occurs first, this section shall apply to any conservatorships established after that date.

Chapter 2

Capacity

While Britney Spears was being held at U.C.L.A. Medical Center, the conservatorship attorneys needed one more document to seal the deal on the then-temporary conservatorship. Checking the "dementia" box on the conservatorship form was not quite enough to meet the court's standards for giving dad Jamie Spears full legal and physical control of his daughter and her property.

The orders for the conservatorship, as well as court-appointed counsel, all hinged on whether Britney had the mental capacity to care for herself, manage her own money and property, and choose her own lawyer. A capacity declaration from a physician was the primary basis for determining a proposed conservatee's mental capacities. These reports would be sealed from the general public to protect a proposed conservatee's medical privacy. Although sealed documents are unavailable for public access, every document filed with the court is logged in the public record.

The attorneys on the case detailed the work they did over the weekend in their declarations filed at Los Angeles Superior Court on Monday, February 4, 2008. They saw, called, and emailed several attorneys who represented Britney in other cases.

Jeryll Cohen wrote,

> On Friday, February 1, 2008, following receipt of
> certified copies of the orders appointing temporary

conservators and letters of temporary conservatorship for both Britney's estate and person (respectively, the "Orders" and the "Letters'"), I returned directly to my office. I arrived there at approximately 5:15 p.m. I am informed and believe that Andrew Wallet, co-conservator of Britney's estate, called Ronald Rale, an attorney at Trope & Trope, to inform him of the appointment of Mr. Spears and Mr. Wallet in the conservatorship. I am further informed and believe that upon Mr. Wallet's receipt of the Orders and Letters sent to him by a colleague of mine at Luce Forward, he forwarded the Orders and Letters to Mr. Rale.

While there were many tasks to accomplish to implement the conservatorship—most urgently, securing Britney's Beverly Hills home and vehicles and making arrangements with UCLA Medical Center (where Britney is currently a patient) for the probate investigator to visit Britney that evening—I obtained contact information for the two lawyers at Trope & Trope whom I understand are in charge of Britney's representation in the family law matter regarding custody of her children. I contacted the home and work telephone numbers for Anne Kiley and the work telephone number for Sorrell Trope. I called all of those numbers and left a message on each voice mail informing them of the content of the portions of the Orders and Letters pertaining to the family law matter, and I gave them my cell phone number and asked them to call me to coordinate the representation of Britney, most particularly because of the hearing scheduled for 8:30 a.m. on Monday, February 4, 2008.

At approximately 5:00 p.m. on Sunday, February 3, 2008, I sent an e-mail to Anne Kiley, an attorney at Trope & Trope involved in Britney's representation in the family law matter, requesting that the Trope & Trope attorneys contact me.

I received no contact from Mr. Trope or Ms. Kiley until I received an e-mail from Ms. Kiley at 8:20 p.m. on Sunday, February 3, 2008 informing me that she had been out of town and was not available to talk until 6:45 a.m. on Monday, February 4, 2008. I did speak with her this morning, on February 4, before the Family Court hearing.

I am informed and believe that at approximately 9 a.m. on Saturday, February 2, 2008, medical personnel at UCLA Medical Center informed my colleague Geraldine A. Wyle, a partner at Luce Forward also representing Mr. Spears, that a young lawyer, later identified as Tara Scott of Trope & Trope, had already been at the hospital for some time waiting to see Britney. I am further informed that Britney was initially unresponsive to Ms. King's [sic] request and finally, after Ms. Scott visited for a very short while, Britney stated that she was too tired to talk.

I am informed that medical personnel at UCLA Medical Center told my colleague, Vivian Thoreen, an associate at Luce Forward also representing Mr. Spears, on

February 2, 2008 that the attorney who sought to visit Britney on Saturday, February 2, 2008 was Ms. Scott.

I am further informed and believe that Ms. Thoreen telephoned Mr. Rale on the morning of Saturday, February 2, 2008, to confirm whether or not he was an attorney at the law firm of Trope & Trope. I am informed and believe that Ms. Thoreen had a pleasant conversation with Mr. Rale.

At approximately 12:58 p.m. on Saturday, February 2, 2008, Ms. Wyle and Ms. Thoreen received an e-mail communication from Adam Streisand, a partner at Loeb & Loeb LLP, that mischaracterized the conversation between Ms. Thoreen and Mr. Rale and accused Mr. Spears of attempting "nothing more than a hostile takeover of our client [Britney] for improper purposes."

Ms. Wyle forwarded the e-mail to me and, at approximately 2:52 p.m. on Saturday, February 2, 2008, I e-mailed Mr. Streisand, suggesting that we all "put our heads together and come up with the best and least ugly way to save this young woman's life, bring her back to her babies and keep her safe from predators. ¶ Please call me." Mr. Streisand's response, more than 24 hours later, was to make a demand for his immediate provision of the petitions for the two conservatorships for Britney. The email correspondence I exchanged with Mr. Streisand is attached collectively as Exhibit A. At the time of my execution of this declaration, I am still unaware of any authority Mr. Streisand has to demand those documents.

I am informed and believe that Ms. Thoreen left a voicemail for PVP counsel, Samuel Ingham III at approximately 7:30 p.m. on Saturday, February 2, 2008, and then had a telephone conversation with him at approximately 11:00 a.m. on Sunday, February 3, 2008, wherein she informed him that she had arranged for him to see Britney at UCLA Medical Center. I am further informed and believe that Mr. Ingham later informed Ms. Thoreen that he had visited Britney on the afternoon of Sunday, February 3, 2008.

<u>Exhibit A, email response to Adam Streisand</u>

From: Cohen, Jeryll
Sent: Saturday, February 02, 2008 2:52 PM
To: 'astreisand@XXXXXXX'
Cc: Thoreen, Vivian; Wyle, Geraldine
Subject: Britney

Adam,

Let's talk. I understand you feel you have certain obligations, but you are a father too. Let's see if we can all put our heads together and come up with the best and least ugly way to save this young woman's life, bring her back to her babies and keep her safe from predators.

Please call me [REDACTED]

Best regards,
Jeryll

Vivian Thoreen's statement gave a timeline of her Saturday snooping around at U.C.L.A. Medical Center, as well as further communication with Mr. Streisand:

> On the morning of February 2, 2008, I learned that an attorney from Trope & Trope, who I later learned that day from medical personnel was Tara Scott, had tried to visit Britney at UCLA Medical Center earlier that morning on Saturday, February 2, 2008. At approximately 11:30 a.m. on February 2, I telephoned Ronald Rale of Trope & Trope. He had previously been with another law firm, and I wanted to confirm whether or not he had returned to the law firm of Trope & Trope. He confirm ed that he had. I had a pleasant conversation with Mr. Rale.
>
> After my telephone conversation with Mr. Rale concluded, I went to UCLA Medical Center, and was there from approximately 1:00 p.m. to 6:30 p.m.
>
> At approximately 12:58 p.m. on Saturday, February 2, 2008, my colleague Geraldine A. Wyle, a partner at Luce Forward who also represents Mr. Spears, and I received an e-mail communication from Adam Streisand, a partner at Loeb & Loeb LLP, that mischaracterized my conversation with Mr. Rale. That e-mail accused Mr. Spears of attempting "nothing more than a hostile takeover of our client [Britney] for improper purposes." Attached as Exhibit A is a true and correct copy of Mr. Streisand's e-mail communication to Ms. Wyle and me.
>
> While at UCLA Medical Center, I learned from the

medical staff that Ms. Scott had called Britney's treating physician at least three (3) times that day. Ms. Scott never contacted me, and I understand that she did not contact either of my colleagues at Luce Forward, Ms. Wyle or Jeryll Cohen, both of whom represent Mr. Spears also.

At approximately 7:30 p.m. on February 2, I telephoned PVP counsel Samuel D. Ingham III, to let him know that I had made arrangements for him to see Britney at UCLA Medical Center. He was not available, so I left him a voicemail and asked that he call me at his convenience.

At approximately 11:00 a.m. on February 3, I spoke with Mr. Ingham. He confirmed that he had received my voicemail from February 2 and told me that he was in the process of making arrangements to visit with Britney later that day.

Mr. Ingham called me at approximately 5:30 p.m. on Sunday, February 3, 2008 to tell me that he had seen Britney on the afternoon of Sunday, February 3, 2008.

Exhibit A, email from Adam Streisand

From: Adam Streisand [astreisand@XXXXXXXX]
Sent: Saturday, February 02, 2008 12:58 PM
To: Vivian Lee Thoreen
Cc: Geraldine A. Wyle
Subject: Britney Spears

Vivian, am told that you called Ron Rale and told him

that Britney has been adjudged incompetent. That is false and you know it.

You further stated that Mr. Rale has no right to see his client without approval from the temporary conservators. That is also false. Your statements further confirm that this is nothing more than a hostile takeover of our client for improper purposes.

We have every right to see and talk to our client whenever we want without anyone's approval.

Adam F. Streisand
Loeb & Loeb LLP

The February 4 statement from Ms. Wyle concluded with her attempt to secure a capacity declaration about Britney's mental health, but not from her reported treating physician, Dr. Deborah Nadel:

At approximately 9 a.m. on Saturday, February 2, 2008, medical personnel at UCLA Medical Center informed me that a young lawyer, later identified as Tara Scott of Trope & Trope, had already been at the hospital for some time waiting to see Britney. Medical personnel told me that Britney was initially unresponsive to Ms. King's [sic] request and finally, after Ms. Scott visited for a very short while, Britney stated that she was too tired to talk.

At approximately 1:12 p.m. on Saturday, February 2, 2008, my colleague Vivian Thoreen, an associate at Luce Forward also representing Mr. Spears, and I received an e-mail communication from Adam Streisand, a partner at Loeb & Loeb LLP. In response, I sent Mr. Streisand an e-mail inviting him to contact my colleague Jeryll Cohen, a special counsel at Luce Forward also representing Mr. Spears, who would arrange a conference call over the weekend at which we could discuss this matter. Because I was traveling on vacation and was about to enter and remain in an area where I would have no cell phone or e-mail access, I forwarded that e-mail to Ms. Cohen. As I have no e-mail access, I do not know whether Mr. Streisand responded directly to me instead of to Ms. Cohen as I had requested.

In the early afternoon of Saturday, February 2, 2008, I contacted Dr. James Long, a psychiatrist who had treated Britney at some point in 2007 and has had some reporting function to the family law court, the details of which I am unaware. I informed Dr. Long of the orders appointing temporary conservators and letters of temporary conservatorship for both Britney's estate and person and told him that, while Dr. Long was under no order to provide a capacity declaration, Mr. Spears had been informed by the Court that he needed to provide a capacity declaration so that the Court could make necessary determinations relating to the conservatorships. I informed Dr. Long that I would try to reach him over the weekend. I left a message on Dr. Long's office voice mail on the evening of Saturday, February 2, 2008 and then paged him late in the morning on Sunday, February 3, 2008. Dr. Long promptly returned the page and told me that he had been instructed by his attorney not to discuss the matter with me. I requested that Dr. Long ask his attorney to call me and provided my telephone number at the hotel at which I am staying. I received a telephone message from the hotel receptionist stating that Dr. Long had called the main number and asked the receptionist to give me the message that neither Dr. Long nor his counsel may speak with me.

The conservatorship attorneys had around 24 hours—between Dr. Long's rejection after late Sunday morning and the hearing on Monday at 1:30 p.m.—to find an accredited doctor, have them meet with Britney to perform an evaluation, write up a capacity declaration, and file it at Stanley Mosk Courthouse.

The declarations filed on Monday, February 4 came from James P. Spears and attorneys Geraldine A. Wyle, Vivian Lee Thoreen, and Jeryll S. Cohen. They hadn't managed to get a capacity declaration to the courthouse on time.

Mr. Streisand recounted that morning in the documentary *Framing Britney Spears:*

> The day I went to court for her [Britney Spears], the judge [Reva Goetz] said, "I've got a medical report, and you haven't seen it, Mr. Streisand, and I'm not gonna show it to you. And it shows that she's not capable of retaining counsel and directing counsel on her own." (Day, 2021)

In the official Minutes entered for the February 4 hearing, there was no mention of a capacity report or any doctor who might have written one or given testimony. There was nothing to substantiate claims of incapacity:

SUPERIOR COURT OF CALIFORNIA,

COUNTY OF LOS ANGELES

Date: February 4, 2008

HONORABLE: REVA GOETZ
COMMISSIONER A. MURDOCK, DEPUTY COURT CLERK
SHERIFF TAMARA VOGL CSR #10186

BP-108870

SPEARS BRITNEY JEAN - CONSERVATORSHIP

COUNSEL FOR PETITIONER:
See below for all appearances

COUNSEL FOR OBJECTOR:
See below for all appearances

NATURE OF PROCEEDINGS: PETITION FOR APPOINTMENT OF TEMPORARY CONSERVATOR OF THE PERSON AND THE ESTATE

Matter is called for hearing, continued from February 1, 2008.

Jeffrey D. Wexler, Jeryll S. Cohen, and Vivian Lee Thoreen appear on behalf of petitioner James P. Spears.

Samuel D. Ingham III, court appointed PVP, appears on behalf of Britney Spears.

Andrew M. Wallet appears on behalf of himself as co-conservator of the estate.

Adam F. Streisand appears on behalf of Britney Spears.

Testimony is taken.

Application to Seal Records re Conservatorship of the Person is granted as to documents protected under Cal. R. Court 2.550(d) and under HIPPA [sic] related to medical records. The court record is sealed under HIPPA regarding discussions made related to the medical issues. Request to seal financial records will require its own separate motion.

Howard Grossman is sworn and testifies.

Proceedings are ordered closed to address the medical issues. Court and counsels address Mr. Streisand's authority to remain during the closed proceedings. Mr. Streisand is excluded after being heard. Court finds that Ms. Spears had no capacity to retain Mr. Streisand.

PVP advised his client of today's proceedings and waives her appearance for today.

PVP shall accept service on his client's behalf.

PVP's request for the court to retain an expert pursuant to Evidence Code 730 and suggestion of Dr. Steven (Stephen ?)[sic] Marmer is heard and granted. PVP shall contact Mr. [sic] Marmer to ascertain his willingness and availability. Mr. Marmer shall file a report by February 13, 2008, if not sooner, re Ms. Spears 1) capacity to participate in the Conservatorship proceedings, 2) ability to manage her financial affairs, 3) ability to retain and direct counsel, and/or 4) her susceptibility to undue influence. Mr. Marmer's reports shall also address the possibility for psychotropic medication for Ms. Spears.

The report shall not be made available to anyone without a court order except the following: Samuel Ingham PVP, counsels for petitioner, Mr. Wallet, and the Court.

Court makes additional orders related to the appointment of the Temporary Conservator of the Person and/or Estate, as more fully reflected in the official notes of the court reporter and incorporated herein by reference, and the orders will be reflected in the attorney order.

The civil harassment restraining order (form CH-120) is modified by the Court, as agreed by all counsels, on page 1 of 4 of the original by marking and [sic] "x" at item 4b. Counsels for petitioner receive copies.

Temporary letters, with additional orders made today, are extended to February 14, 2008.

THIS MATTER IS CONTINUED TO FEBRUARY 14, 2008 AT 1:30 P.M. IN DEPARTMENT 9.

Ms. Spears shall not have any contact direct or indirect which includes text messaging and e-mails with Osama (Sam) Lutfi.

Proceedings remained closed until concluded.

Court makes additional orders as more fully reflected in the official notes of the court reporter and incorporated herein by reference.

Counsel for petitioner shall prepare the order.

Following the February 4 hearing, the conservatorship attorneys wrote up Orders from that hearing for Judge Goetz to

sign off on on February 6. In these orders, Dr. J. Edward Spar's declaration entered the records. It was listed as a document distinct from those filed in the case:

> As a result of the pleadings that have been filed, the declaration by J. Edward Spar, M.D., and the Report of PVP counsel Mr. Ingham, the court finds that Ms. Spears does not have the capacity to retain counsel and she lacked the capacity to retain Adam F. Streisand as her counsel.

The declaration was then referenced two more times:

> Ms. Spears has a right to be present at this hearing, and she is not present. According to Dr. Spar's declaration, Ms. Spears does not have the ability to attend the hearing. Mr. Ingham indicated in his Report that Ms. Spears was given an opportunity through him to communicate to this Court, and she has elected not to. On the basis of Dr. Spar's declaration and Mr. Ingham's Report, the Court should waive Ms. Spears' presence at the hearing.

During the February 4 hearing, Mr. Ingham requested an Evidence Code 730 report about Britney. This would be different from Dr. Spar's declaration referenced on February 6.

In the context of a conservatorship, a "730 report" was typically based on an evaluation of a conservatee. This evidence would inform the Court's judgment about the health—both physical and mental—of a conservatee.

Court records showed that Mr. Ingham did file "First Report of PVP Attorney" under seal on February 14—the day after Dr. Marmer's 730 report was expected.

In the documentary *Britney vs Spears*, the hosts shared a

document that they asserted someone leaked to them. It was dated March 5, 2008 and addressed to Mr. Ingham. The report stated, "This is a follow-up progress report on the condition of Ms. Britney Spears". (Carr, 2021)

Court records show that Mr. Ingham did file "Second Report of PVP Attorney" under seal on March 7. Although either of those reports could mention Britney's mental capacity, neither was at Stanley Mosk Courthouse on February 4.

Dr. Spar was interviewed for the documentary *Britney vs Spears*. Following confidentiality guidelines, he refused to state whether he had ever met Britney. The director, Erin Lee Carr, pressed him about finding his name in the records of Britney's case:

> Ms. Carr: Here is a court document, said, "According to Dr. Spar's declaration." *Hands paper to Dr. Spar.*
>
> Dr. Spar: Okay, again, show me my signed declaration. If you show me a public document with my signature on it, I will verify my signature. Other than that, I'm not gonna talk about whether anybody ever retained me to see anybody; not just Britney Spears. These are all confidential evaluations.
>
> (Carr, 2021)

Of course, she couldn't meet that requirement to get his verification. The public only has the claims of the people who were present at the beginning of the conservatorship and made reference to the phantom declaration later on.

For example, the conservators thought it appropriate to respond to a lawsuit against Britney by referencing Dr. Spar's capacity declaration—a document that wasn't in the court records.

On October 27, 2007, Wright Entertainment Group filed a lawsuit in Florida regarding a contract dispute with Britney Spears and Britney Touring, Inc.[1] They subpoenaed financial documents and testimony from Britney, and requested a jury trial to determine how much money they were still owed.

Once the conservators entered the picture in 2008, they provided the letters of conservatorship as evidence that Britney was not competent to participate in the litigation.

In Wright's April 14, 2008 opposition to the defendants' response, they argued,

> Defendants' Motion presents no evidence of incompetence except the conservatorship orders. The second order, filed February 6, 2008 (Exhibit "O"), extended the conservatorship to February 14, 2008 and expanded it to cover all litigation, but no one informed the Plaintiffs, who had Final Judgments entered on February 14, 2008. This order references the declaration of Dr. J. Evan [sic] Spar relating to capacity, but no report has been provided (Exhibit "O" 7 & 8).

Wright never got Britney to sit for a deposition. At the end of December 2008, the original judge presiding over the suit was replaced by Judge Thomas Smith. Judge Smith was obliged to disclose that he had previously worked at Holland & Knight, the firm that was representing the conservators in Wright's suit. On July 7, 2009, after mediation, Judge Smith dismissed the case with prejudice. The parties had settled, everyone would pay their own legal costs, and Wright agreed to not sue over this

---

[1] Wright Entertainment Group, LLC & Wright Entertainment Group, Inc. vs. Britney Spears & Britney Touring, Inc., 9th Jud. Cir. Ct., Orange Cnty., FL. Case 48-2007-CA-014233-0.

again.

Ultimately, when Judge Brenda Penny terminated the conservatorship on November 12, 2021, she stated,

> In this case, the Court finds that this was a voluntary conservatorship, that there was no capacity declaration filed stating that Britney Spears lacked capacity, and therefore, there is no need for a submission by her of a capacity declaration stating that she has capacity for the Court to consider in making an order terminating the conservatorship.

Chapter 3

Representation

Judge Reva Goetz granted conservator Jamie Spears "the power to restrict visitors" on February 6, 2008. This included restricting meetings with attorneys other than Samuel Ingham. After Adam Streisand's ejection from the February 4 hearing, Britney Spears continued reaching out for legal support.

One such attorney was Gary Stiffelman, who had been Britney's entertainment lawyer. His declaration to Los Angeles Superior Court signed February 13, 2008 mentioned her calls:

> I have received several telephone calls from Ms. Spears over the last several days. I spoke with her on Wednesday, February 6, and have spoken with her at least twice during the last few days, on Saturday, February 9 and again on Monday, February 11 when she placed calls to me. The caller information on my telephone indicated that Ms. Spears called me from more than one telephone number over that time period. Due to the attorney-client communications privilege, I am not revealing the content of our conversations.

Just four days before Britney's second involuntary hold, attorney Jon Eardley reached out to her via FedEx. His letter was included as evidence in a January 30, 2009 temporary restraining order request from Jamie's attorneys. Mr. Eardley express-ed sympathy and talked up his capabilities:

> I have developed a legal strategy for you that I am confident will turn everything around, and ultimately garner you [Britney] **full custody** of your children within approximately 30 to 60 days. [emphasis supplied] I am a father of two girls, ages 3 and a half and one and can only imagine the heartbreak you are going through.
>
> After having practiced law for years in Los Angeles, I find myself, at many times sickened by the corruption of the downtown court system. However, your case is the worst I have ever seen because they are unabated in the systematic destruction of your character and reputation; and they will not be happy until they have denied you your freedom and milked you for your last dime. The custody case, as you know, is nothing more than a flat out extortion scheme, with your children being used as pawns.

Mr. Eardley insisted that he would volunteer his time and was "not interested in publicity, money, or anything other than seeing you obtain full custody of your children." However, he repeatedly wrote with animosity about her ex-husband's attorney and the corrupt downtown court system. He aimed to get both her ex-husband's attorney and the commissioner adjudicating the case disqualified from working on the case.

On February 14, the date when the temporary conservatorships were scheduled to expire, Mr. Eardley filed a notice to remove the conservatorship case to a federal court to consider whether the conservators had violated federal laws:

> Please take notice that the removing party, Britney J. Spears, hereby removes in its entirety to this court the

state court action described above, as the Conservatorship of Britney Jean Spears, with the Los Angeles Superior Court case number BP 108870.

Ms. Spears has not received the benefit of a single hearing before the court; yet she has been stripped of her right to access counsel of her choosing and to meet with her counsel in a private meeting.

Mr. Eardley's claims were based in part on the powers Judge Goetz granted to Jamie in early February. His concerns included medical care, the child custody case, and other violations of Britney's constitutionally-protected rights. However, his primary argument wasn't about those rights. Mr. Eardley instead focused on a federal law about medication:

This action is a civil action of which this court has original jurisdiction pursuant to the provisions of 28 U.S.C. § 1441 (b) in that it is a civil action that touches upon important issues of federal law, to wit whether an adult child may be subjected by her parents to their complete and total control in that the petitioner and conservator supplements the medications scheduled under the Food, Drug, and Cosmetics Act, 21 U.S.C. § 301 et seq., and prescribed to her by her doctors with a near total deprivation of civil rights.

Jamie's attorneys filed a response five days later. They countered Mr. Eardley's claims and requested the case be remanded to the probate court. The conservatorship team maintained that Britney lacked capacity to hire an attorney of her choice. They also insisted that Jamie couldn't have done something he wasn't allowed to do:

The allegation that is the centerpiece of Mr. Eardley's claim for federal question jurisdiction—his allegation that Mr. Spears "supplements" Britney's medications—disregards the fact that the Probate Court has *not* granted Mr. Spears medical powers and that medications therefore do not fall within the scope of the conservatorship. [emphasis supplied]

Judge Philip Gutierrez agreed that the case should be remanded to the state probate court where it originated:

> On **Feb. 14, 2008**, this action was removed to this Court pursuant to 28 U.S.C. § 1441.
>
> However, the jurisdictional allegations appear to be defective for the reason(s) opposite the box(es) checked: Removal is on the basis of federal question jurisdiction pursuant to 28 U.S.C. § 1331 but it appears that the claims may not "arise under" federal law.
> [X] The Court notes the following potential procedural defect(s):
> [X] the removing defendant(s) did not attach to the notice of removal a copy of all process, pleadings, and orders served on the defendant(s). 28 U.S.C. § 1446(a).
>
> Accordingly, the Court orders defendant(s) to show cause in writing no later than Friday **Feb. 29, 2008** why this action should not be remanded for the reasons noted above. This deadline shall not extend the time for responding to any motion for remand filed by Plaintiff(s). Plaintiff(s) may submit a response in the same time period. Plaintiff(s) must submit a response within 30

days of the date of removal if the defects are procedural and plaintiff(s) object(s) and request(s) remand. See 28 U.S.C. § 1447(c). The parties are reminded that courtesy copies are to be delivered to Chambers. Failure of defendant(s) to respond by the above date will result in the Court **remanding** this action to state court.

Since stretching the definition of "supplement" of a medication to include "deprivation of civil rights" hadn't worked, Mr. Eardley listed more conventional rights in his February 25 response to the judge's order. That was not enough to overcome the fact that Britney couldn't hire him. Ultimately, Judge Gutierrez did not rule on the substance of Mr. Eardley's arguments. He maintained his order of February 19 that the case be remanded to the state court:

> As previously stated by this Court's order, Jon Eardley has no authority to act on behalf of Britney Jean Spears. Further filings by Mr. Eardley in this matter that purport to be on behalf of Britney Jean Spears will warrant sanctions.

In January 2009, Mr. Eardley was served with a temporary restraining order on behalf of Britney through Jamie. Along with Sam Lutfi and Adnan Ghalib, Mr. Eardley was ordered to stay at least 250 feet away from and avoid contact with not only Britney but her two sons and parents.

In addition to standard restraining order limitations, these orders included:

> You are prohibited from: (1) acting on Ms. Spears' behalf, or purporting to act on her behalf; (2) inducing or assisting any other person to take action on Ms. Spears'

behalf, or to purport to take action on her behalf; and (3) filing, or inducing or assisting any other person to file, legal pleadings that purport to be filed on Ms. Spears' behalf.

On January 27, 2009, attorney John Anderson sent documents to the co-conservators' lawyers, Geraldine Wyle and Jeryll Cohen, about Britney hiring him to replace Mr. Ingham. Mr. Anderson followed up with a phone call to their firm, Luce Forward, and spoke with attorney Jeffrey Wexler.

In a statement in support of the January 2009 restraining order against Messrs. Lutfi, Eardley, and Ghalib, Mr. Wexler recalled,

> Mr. Anderson said that he was initially contacted by attorney Jon Eardley, who had asked him for his expertise in helping Mr. Eardley to decide what documents he would be able to file on behalf of conservatee Britney Jean Spears ("Ms. Spears"). Mr. Anderson told me that he had been contacted by Mr. Eardley about three or four weeks ago, and that he had spoken with him a couple times.

> Mr. Anderson said that he was thereafter contacted by Sam Lutfi, who said that Ms. Spears wanted to retain an attorney but was not allowed to speak to one. Mr. Anderson said that he had spoken with Mr. Lutfi about two or three weeks later.

> Mr. Anderson said that he told Mr. Lutfi that he would not talk to Ms. Spears unless he received documents with her signature. Mr. Anderson told me that he had prepared a petition, engagement letter, and related

papers and sent them to Mr. Lutfi, and that Mr. Lutfi thereafter returned signed versions of those documents to him.

I explained to Mr. Anderson that the Court had found in February 2008 that Ms. Spears lacks capacity to hire counsel. I also told Mr. Anderson that in February 2008 Mr. Eardley had filed papers removing the conservatorship proceedings to the United States District Court for the Central District of California, and that the Central District had subsequently remanded the case on the grounds that Ms. Spears lacks capacity to hire counsel and that Mr. Eardley therefore was not authorized to file the notice of removal on her behalf.

I also told Mr. Anderson that on October 28, 2008 the Court had granted the Co-Conservators' *ex parte* application for a protective order against a deposition of Ms. Spears noticed by the plaintiffs in a Florida lawsuit.[1]

Mr. Anderson told me on January 27, 2009 that he had not yet filed the *ex parte* application and related papers with the Court. In our conversation and in two e-mails that he sent me later that day, Mr. Anderson agreed that he would not file his *ex parte* papers on Thursday, January 29, 2009, and that he would not file them at all pending his further investigation of the issues.

On January 27, 2009, I e-mailed Mr. Anderson certain publicly filed pleadings and orders related to the Court's

---

[1] *See* Chapter 2: Capacity

finding as to lack of capacity.

In a telephone conversation on January 29, 2009, Mr. Anderson told Ms. Wyle and me that he had sent e-mails to Mr. Lutfi and Mr. Eardley telling him that he had a conflict and would have no further involvement with the matter.

Chapter 4

Come Back

In February 2008, Judge Reva Goetz ordered that Britney Spears was so gravely disabled that she lacked the capacity to feed, dress, and house herself. In March 2008, she performed in the first of two episodes of the sitcom *How I Met Your Mother*. The work continued throughout the first year of the conservatorship, including the production of an album in between live performances and TV appearances.

March

- *How I Met Your Mother* TV show episode "Ten Sessions"

May

- *How I Met Your Mother* TV show episode "Everything Must Go"

September

- *MTV Video Music Awards* live TV special

November

- *MTV Europe Music Awards* live TV special
- *Britney: For the Record* documentary
- *Madonna: Sticky & Sweet Tour*, "Human Nature"
- "Womanizer" music video

- *Circus* international promotional tour
- *The X Factor UK* TV show

December

- *Circus* album release
- "Circus" music video
- *Good Morning America* TV magazine
- *The Ellen DeGeneres Show* TV show episode #6.71
- *Christmas in Rockefeller Center* TV special

Chapter 5

Estate

In 2004, Britney Spears took steps to protect her assets by setting up her own trust:

ASSIGNMENT TO THE SJB REVOCABLE TRUST DATED JULY 26, 2004

I, BRITNEY JEAN SPEARS, hereby assign to myself, as the sole Trustee of the SJB REVOCABLE TRUST, dated July 26, 2004, all of my right, title, and interest in and to all of my property, of whatsoever kind and character, including, without limitation, all of my right, title, and interest in and to all of the following:

1. My furniture and furnishings, clothing, jewelry, vehicles and accessories to vehicles, books, paintings and other artwork, and other tangible articles of a personal, domestic, household, or recreational use or nature, together with any insurance on such property.

2. My stocks and securities of every kind and character.

3. My cash and cash equivalents, including all bank and savings accounts of every kind and character.

This Assignment was executed by me this day, July 26, 2004, at Los Angeles, California, and is effective immediately.

//bjs//
BRITNEY JEAN SPEARS

The SJB Trust was not initially part of the conservatorship of Britney's estate. However, once Britney was deemed incapable of managing her own estate and person, the successor co-trustees stepped up to manage the trust on her behalf. Those successors were Bryan Spears, Britney's older brother, and Ivan Taback, the attorney who originally drafted the trust. On March 17, 2008, they filed a petition in Los Angeles Superior Court to confirm their control of the business entities held in the trust:

PETITION FOR ORDER CONFIRMING TITLE
TO TRUST PROPERTY
(Probate Code § 850(a)(3))

The Trust. BRITNEY JEAN SPEARS ("Britney"), as Settlor and initial trustee, established The SJB Revocable Trust under a Declaration of Trust dated July 26, 2004. The Trust is a "Revocable Living Trust," established by Britney to hold and manage her material financial assets during her lifetime, and to provide for the distribution of those assets upon her death.

Britney Ceased To Act As Trustee. Pursuant to Orders of this Court first entered February 1, 2008, a Conservator was appointed for Britney's Person, and Co-Conservators were appointed for Britney's Estate. In a related proceeding, by Order of this Court entered February 14, 2008, the Court determined that Britney had ceased to act as Trustee of the Trust.

Successor Trustees. Pursuant to the terms of the Trust, Petitioners became Temporary Successor Co-Trustees of the Trust when Britney ceased to act as Trustee. On February 14, 2008, the Court entered its Order appointing Petitioners as Temporary Successor Co-Trustees of the Trust and Petitioners have been acting as Temporary Successor Co-Trustees of the Trust since such date.

Britney's Legal Entities. Petitioners seek this Court's Order confirming that the Trust owns all right, title, and interest previously vested in Britney in and to the following entities:

BBS Entertainment, Inc., Britney Brands, Inc., Britney Films, Ltd., Britney On-Line, Inc., Britney Television, LLC, One More Time Music, Inc., Parklane Productions, LLC, Coastal Operatives, LLC, B & L Music Inc., Fairy Zone Productions, Inc. (California), Bridgemore Timber, LLC, Vista Peace Productions, LLC, and Britney Touring, Inc. (the "Entities").

Rather than operating the business entities from within the trust, as Britney had, Bryan and Mr. Taback transferred the businesses to the estate. Beginning with Britney Touring, Inc. a month into the conservatorship, the co-conservators of the estate gained control of all the businesses. Some were eventually dissolved and some new ones created, with assets moving between companies over the years:

Subsequent Transfer of Britney Touring, Inc.
On March 10, 2008, the Co-Trustees assigned to Andrew D. Wallet, Esq. and James P. Spears, in their capacities as

Co-Conservators of Britney's Estate, all of the Trust's right, title and interest in and to Britney Touring, Inc. This assignment was made because Petitioners, as Co-Trustees, and the Co-Conservators of Britney's Estate determined jointly that it would be in the best interests of the Trust, the Conservatorship Estate, and Britney, for the Co-Conservators of the Estate to own and control Britney Touring, Inc.

The business entities under the control of the co-conservators included:
- Atara Tours, Inc.
- Bellatori Tours, Inc. *(with Louise Taylor)*
- Brandcasting Unlimited, LLC
- Britney Films, Ltd.
- Britney Brands, Inc.
- Domestic Relations, LLC
- Fairy Zone Productions, Inc.
- One More Time Music, Inc.
- Magnolia Publishing, Inc.
- Miss Britney Recording, Inc.
- Shiloh Standing, Inc.
- Spears Management, Inc.
- Till The World Ends, Inc.
- White Transport, LLC

The addresses for each of the above entities were the addresses of the California and Tennessee offices of Tri Star Sports and Entertainment Group, run by President and CEO Louise "Lou" Taylor. Ms. Taylor was by the Spears family's side throughout the initiation of Britney's conservatorships in 2008 and was hired as her business manager in 2009. In her memoir, mom Lynne Spears explained that Ms. Taylor advised Jamie while he and his attorneys planned the conservatorships.

(Craker & Spears, 2008) Ms. Taylor and Tri Star continued managing the businesses and finances of Britney's estate until abruptly resigning in October 2020.[1]

Typical tasks of the business manager of an artist's estate included tracking payments and expenses related to intellectual property, including royalties on songwriting and licensing of merchandise. While preparing the accounting for 2010, the co-conservators of the estate petitioned Judge Reva Goetz to make the annual accounting more opaque. On March 16, 2010, Judge Goetz ordered the appraisal of Britney's intellectual property be waived:

> The Intellectual Property rights of the Conservatee shall not be appraised by the probate referee; rather the Petitioners shall list the entities owned by the Conservatee on Attachment No. 1 of the Inventory and Appraisal Patrial No. 2, and designate at the value of the entities the balance of cash on hand in each of the entities at the time of the establishment of the Conservatorship without indicating the value of any intellectual property owned by the Conservatee.

Starting with the 2010 accounting and continuing from then on, the annual account included the footnote, "Due to the difficulties in valuing the Conservatee's Intellectual Property, including without limitation, trademarks, royalties, copyrights, name and likeness, these assets are not valued at this time pursuant to Order of the Court filed 3/16/2010."

Judge Goetz's order allowed the co-conservators to keep the details of payments to the estate for any intellectual

---

[1] *See* Chapter 14: Dissipate

property out of the official court record. The data would not even be included in redacted form. The obligations of the co-conservators and business manager were limited to the total assets of all business entities combined at the beginning of the year and the total assets remaining at the end of the year. Judge Goetz determined that information about how much money the businesses had earned and spent throughout the year was unnecessary when reporting on the assets of the estate.

By the time the Twelfth Accounting was filed in 2020, reporting on the funds of the business entities from the previous year was whittled down to three lines (plus footnotes):

PROPERTY ON HAND AT BEGINNING OF
ACCOUNT PERIOD
JANUARY 1, 2019

Investment in Business Assets† (at Appraisal Values)	Estimated Market Value	Carry Value
100% Interest in Entity No. 10	$ 4,302,235.62	$ 8,106,628.47
100% Interest in Entity No. 1	$ 15,088.56	$ 525,046.39
100% Interest in Entity No. 2	$ 30,264.17	$ 41,684.06

† This schedule reflects initial inventory values only. It does not reflect the actual balance of cash on hand at the beginning of the account period.

i With respect to values indicated for carry values and market values, the Co-Conservators are relying on the business manager's records and have not verified the values reflected.

Chapter 6

Compensation

The California Probate Code regulations on probate conservatorships did not specify limits on how much conservators were paid for their services. Code 2640 (c) (1) vaguely stated that compensation was what "the court determines is just and reasonable". This could include both a fee for labor and reimbursement of costs.

Regulations specified that not all conservator legal fees could be paid from the conservatee's estate:

> California Probate Code 2640. (d) Notwithstanding the provisions of subdivision (c), the guardian or conservator shall not be compensated from the estate for any costs or fees that the guardian or conservator incurred in unsuccessfully opposing a petition, or other request or action, made by or on behalf of the ward or conservatee, unless the court determines that the opposition was made in good faith, based on the best interests of the ward or conservatee.

> California Probate Code 2647. No attorney fees may be paid from the estate of the ward or conservatee without prior court order. The estate of the ward or conservatee is not obligated to pay attorney fees established by any engagement agreement or other contract until it has been approved by the court. This does not preclude an

award of fees by the court pursuant to this chapter even if the contractual obligations are unenforceable pursuant to this section.

The initial "just and reasonable" compensation that Judge Reva Goetz agreed to was listed in details of the accounting on how Britney Spears's money was spent during the first year of the conservatorship. Over a quarter of the total expenses for the year went to conservatorship costs. In 2008, expenses for the conservators, their conservatorship-related legal costs and fees, and the attorney appointed to represent her totaled $2,761,113.66. She was allowed $55,500 of her own money, as detailed in the First Accounting filed in 2009:

C-2 Conservatee's Residential Expenses	$ 953,236.79
C-3 Fiduciary & Attorney Fees	
Co-Conservator - James Spears	$ 168,790.00
Co-Conservator - Andrew Wallet	$ 409,849.26
Co-Conservator - Spears' Legal Representation	$ 1,053,810.00
Conservatee's Attorneys' Fees - Samuel D. Ingham III	$ 405,990.64
Co-Conservators' Legal Fees	$ 610,308.88
Co-Conservator's Legal Costs	$ 112,364.88
Kevin Federline	$ 625,000.00
Royalty Audit	$ 11,171.25
Business Management & Accounting	$ 355,947.26
TOTAL	$ 3,753,232.17
C-5 Living Expenses	$ 137,554.80
C-9 Business Expenses	$ 1,868,551.49

C-10 Personnel and Assistants	$	186,555.77
C-11 Automobile Expenses	$	29,932.72
C-12: Advances to Entities		
Advances to Entities	$	726,482.85
(See Schedule filed under Seal)		
SJB Revocable Trust	$	18,628.21
(Auto Expenses)	$	745,111.06
C-13: Other Expenses		
Bond Payments	$	750.00
Payments to Conservatee	$	55,500.00
Credit Card Payments	$	128,369.67
Gifts	$	2,887.00
TOTAL	$	187,506.67
C-14: Bank	$	100,371.51

Jamie Spears's compensation for his work as Britney's conservator began accruing on the first day of the conservatorship on February 1, 2008. In his June 6, 2008 petition for payment, he described his labors managing her life during the period of February 1 through March 3, 2008 (except for barbecuing on Super Bowl Sunday):

> Generally speaking, from February 1, 2008 through March 3, 2008, I was with Britney on a near twenty-four-hour basis to ensure her safety and well-being. During the times that I was not with her, I was arranging, coordinating, or managing her medical and legal affairs in addition to addressing other conservatorship issues, as further discussed below. Throughout the time period, I ran errands, including buying groceries and cooking supper on a regular basis. I talked frequently with Britney about her health status. [REDACTED] I arranged

for Britney's transport and security [REDACTED] to go shopping, and so that she could teach a dance class to children. I visited Britney's children and their father, Mr. Federline. I consulted with my attorneys representing me in the Conservatorship. I organized and reviewed household receipts, and I consulted with Andrew Wallet. I continued to consult with Britney's doctors and home care personnel. I spent a good deal of every day conversing with Britney.

Judge Goetz ordered that Jamie be paid $2,500 per week, approximately $10,000 per month. Beginning in December 2008, his monthly compensation increased to $16,000 plus $1,200 for office space rent. He enriched himself further by directly taking a cut of the profits of his conservatee's earnings. For example, for the *Femme Fatale Tour* in 2011, he requested both 0.95% of the tour's gross as well as 2% of manager Larry Rudolph's commission, as detailed in Jamie's September 12, 2011 *Petition for Allowance of Compensation:*

COMPENSATION REQUEST

Petitioners seek compensation to Mr. Spears, in addition to the compensation Mr. Spears receives in his capacity as Conservator of Britney's Person and Co-Conservator of the Estate, from Till the World Ends, Inc. ("TTWE"), for the services Mr. Spears has been and will be performing in various roles and capacities for the 2011 Femme Fatale Tour. These services for the Femme Fatale Tour are over and above the services he performs as Conservator of the Person and Co-Conservator of the Estate. See Declaration of James P. Spears filed concurrently with this Supplement. The additional compensation requested is as follows: [REDACTED] in the amount of [REDACTED] payable to Mr. Spears by TTWE. Mr. Spears, as well, seeks the court's approval of the agreement between Britney's personal manager Larry Rudolph Management, Inc. and ReignDeer Entertainment Corp. (collectively, "Manager") and Mr. Spears whereby Manager's 10% commission from the Femme Fatale Tour will be shared between them as follows: 8% Manager and 2% Mr. Spears, also payable to each of them by TTWE.

In Jamie's declaration accompanying the request, he explained the many roles beyond conservator that he took on for the tour rather than hiring experienced professionals for those duties:

> I have continued in my duties as Britney's Conservator of the Person and Co-Conservator of the Estate. My duties continue to include overseeing and coordinating all of Britney's medical, health, business, costuming, personal, security, household staff, and legal matters (touching upon entertainment, music, family law litigation, the resolution of numerous disputes, and on-going litigation and conservatorship matters). I manage her security arrangements as Britney must be protected from the paparazzi throughout each one of her daily activities. I estimate that I engage in 200 to 400 communications per day to coordinate all of these matters on behalf of the conservatorship [REDACTED]
>
> I am primarily responsible for structuring and

facilitating Britney's business and leisure activities. I have provided Britney with my support and guidance to the best of my ability.

During 2010, Britney's latest album, Femme Fatale, took shape. The release of the album was announced in late 2010 for March 2011. Britney worked hard in the recording sessions and I oversaw all of the negotiations relating to the production of the CD and production of video support for the CD. Inevitably, Britney's music professional asked whether the Conservators would be willing to mount another tour. As Britney had expressed a desire to tour in support of this record, and was wholeheartedly in favor of it, I spearheaded the exploratory discussions, relying to a great extent on the team of professionals who had made the Circus Tour so successful, and as I did for the Circus Tour, I interfaced among the entertainment professionals, the medical professionals, and the conservatorship in developing a concert tour that would be [REDACTED] financially rewarding [REDACTED] for Britney.

I worked with the music professionals to negotiate an agreement with Live Nation, Inc, the tour promoter, that has proven to be extremely beneficial for Britney. She was guaranteed [REDACTED] for the concert tours in North America, and continuing through Europe and South America, with an additional guarantee totaling [REDACTED] The Tour currently has [REDACTED] in guarantees (before expenses) for 78 shows.

With Mr. Wallet, I created Till the World Ends ("TTWE"), a separate corporate entity, for the tour. Rehearsals began in earnest in the winter of 2011, and after a few promotional performances (the kick-off for the Femme Fatale record) and set up for the tour, the "Femme Fatale" tour (the "Tour") was mounted by June of 2011. We completed the North American leg of the Tour mid-August, completing all of the concerts that were planned, plus nine extension shows. The Tour has been a professional success for Britney and Britney has been substantially engaged with her audience throughout. I was with Britney through the Tour, and planned the Tour so that she could travel with her children during their school's summer vacation. [REDACTED] The children were well cared for throughout the Tour, and Britney was able to and did spend enormous amounts of quality time with them. I coordinated Britney's personal schedule and environment and was the tour manager throughout the Tour. I supervised Britney's arrival at each venue, her experience and accommodations while at each venue, and her departures, all of which I planned and executed to minimize the inevitable stress that exists for any major performer, and most particularly Britney [REDACTED]

The Tour is essentially three legs: the initial leg included North America (just completed); the second leg will include Europe, and the third leg will include South America, where she has never toured before. In order to cut overhead, I did not hire personnel for three positions that existed in the Circus Tour—the tour manager (other than myself) and two assistant managers. Salaries paid to these three positions in the Circus Tour were over [REDACTED]

Although significantly scaled down from the Circus Tour, the Tour faced substantial financial and logistical challenges. The staging required complicated technology and highly skilled performers and technicians. I supervised the financial and logistical management of the Tour, oversaw the extensive logistical issues of setting up, breaking down and moving the Tour, with all of its human and technological components. I oversaw the efforts to obtain sponsorships, which were few in this worsening economy. I also implemented and oversaw stringent financial controls to ensure that the Tour was as fiscally lean as feasible. Managing the finances of the Tour with Lou Taylor of Tri Star Sports & Entertainment Group, we instituted at the Tour's outset the same decision-making protocol, policies, procedures, and purchase order systems for payments and financial approvals implemented during the Circus Tour. We used a qualified purchase order system executed and designed by Tri Star where all vendors were required to submit each expenditure, with an executed Purchase Order, directly to TTWE. All of the Purchase Orders as well as all payments were approved and paid with dual signatures from Andrew Wallet and myself.

During the first leg of the Tour, Lou Taylor of Tri Star Sports and Entertainment, the business manager for the

Tour, and I analyzed the various components of the concert program to reduce the number of Tour employees and production components. We pared the tour company by 10+ employees and cut the amount of equipment and staging props to improve the profitability of the North American Tour, as well as the European and South American legs, with substantial net savings in production and transport costs.

I also scrutinized Live Nation's performance in regard to its contract as concert promoter, working in coordination with the entertainment lawyer. I was the primary interface with the entertainment lawyers and the Tour—from day-to-day issues relating to both employees of the Tour, venues, sponsors and vendors to more global issues that developed.

I tackled the myriad issues that arose in—and between—the 78 concerts. I coordinated with Tri Star to monitor the approved vendors to ensure that the vendors were not under-reporting their sales.

I also scrutinized William Morris' performance in regards to its capacity as an agent, working in coordination with the entertainment lawyers to negotiate with William Morris regarding the numerous issues and disputes that developed regarding Tour sponsorships and William Morris' fulfillment of their duties, reducing their compensation dramatically. These negotiations resulted in a net savings to Britney [REDACTED]

While the Tour is not yet completed, we now have a

rough idea of the financial results of the Tour. In part, as a result of my efforts, the Tour will receive approximately [REDACTED] in guarantees. Ticket sales in the concert world have suffered drastically since the Circus Tour (which barely escaped the ravages of the recession). The new reality requires the artists to discount tickets to maximize revenues and fill the concert spaces. With this Tour, Britney has been no exception to this phenomenon, but her Tour will still net several million dollars to her after expenses.

I am advised that my services to the Circus Tour cover an unprecedented range of activities, as I have performed and will continue to perform until the Tour's conclusion the functions of Tour Manager, Logistics Coordinator, Production Manager and the day-to-day coordinator for Britney and for Management. I am advised that compensation of 0.95% of the Tour's gross guaran-tees (an estimated total [REDACTED] would be reason-able compensation for my efforts and the results that I achieved. Therefore, I request approval of compensation in an amount equal to 0.95% of the Tour's gross guaran-tees (an estimated total as compensation for my efforts relating solely to my services rendered to the Femme Fatale Tour).

My role has expanded to include a significant portion of Larry Rudolph's responsibilities as personal manager, including without limitation many of the responsibilities relating to the Tour as well as the production of the 3 D concert video special Britney filmed in Toronto, Larry

Rudolph has also agreed to divert a portion of his income stream to me as I covered a multitude of management responsibilities and support on the ground, such that we agreed that the 10% commission to which Mr. Rudolph is entitled would be shared between Mr. Rudolph and myself as follows: 8% to Mr. Rudolph and 2% to myself. TTWE will disburse these funds to Mr. Rudolph and me accordingly. I therefore request additional approval for the Co-Conservators to divert the 2% of Mr. Rudolph's income stream to me.

The *Femme Fatale Tour* was estimated to have grossed over $68 million, 2.95% of which added up to over $2 million.

Attorney Andrew Wallet was on the conservatorship team from the beginning. He brought in $409,849 in 2008. By the end of his tenure managing Britney's estate, Mr. Wallet was paid $426,000 per year. After eleven years of service, he received an additional $100,000 at his resignation on March 5, 2019.

While requesting a raise, Mr. Wallet had to come up with good reasons for it. The description of his duties provided a glimpse into the particulars of how Britney's work, businesses, and assets were managed. For example, he petitioned the Court for increased compensation during the first year of the *Piece of Me* residency in Las Vegas on November 20, 2013. Mr. Wallet argued,

> This conservatorship has been extremely challenging where all of Declarant's skills have been called upon to make this conservatorship successful. Declarant does not intend to give the impression that Declarant is solely responsible for the success of the conservatorship. This

conservatorship is and has always been a team effort with everyone playing vital roles. However, Declarant was initially brought into this matter to bring his unique expertise, create stability, bring sound judgment and leadership. Declarant has done those things...

The "bad" and incompetent people previously involved in the Conservatee's personal and business life, have been swept out as a result of Declarant's utilizing and urging the use of various legal actions, his terminating people's employment, resolving disputes, resulting in eliminating liabilities, debts and various threats to the conservatorship estate and the person. It has been a full time job for months at a time in order to get things under control and productive.

By way of example, and not by way of limitation, at the planning stages of the Circus Tour, the Declarant instructed entertainment counsel to spread the risk of the Conservatee failing to fulfill her duties on tour because of some third party providing illegal substances. The financial stakes were high and failure was not an option. Declarant insisted that all contracting parties with the conservatorship estate, (there were hundreds of con-tracts), would sign consents to [REDACTED][1] as long as they were involved with the tour, [REDACTED] agree to liquidated damages and confidentiality

---

[1] Author's note: There were long-standing and widespread rumors that people working with Britney under the conservatorship had to agree to drug tests.

acknowledgements of their responsibilities to have [REDACTED] Declarant was greatly concerned at the planning stages for the Circus Tour, that the many hundreds of vendors, drivers, dancers, hair stylists, performers, etc. could bring financial disaster to the tour by providing illegal substances to the Conservatee. That protective environment involving literally hundreds of people, who also assumed the risk if they acted improperly. That protocol greatly reduced the risk of financial failure and personal harm to the Conservatee. The same protocols were employed for the second tour and now for the Las Vegas residency.

The Conservatee's business activities have greatly accelerated due to her increased well being and her capacity to be more engaged in furthering her career activities. The next several years promise to be very lucrative for the conservatorship estate due to the ever increasing marketing, and related business activities that are now pending or have been recently negotiated. Declarant has never been a figure head or a passive observer in this conservatorship but has always been actively engaged in its management and stability.

Declarant seeks modification of his compensation. The "traditional" conservatorship model of hourly compensation does not work in this matter. This conservatorship should be viewed more as a hybrid business model. If Declarant performed the same services, with the same results, in a business setting, his fees would have been in the millions of dollars.

This conservatorship is undoubtedly one of the most complex and challenging. It is atypical. This conservatorship has gone far beyond the norm and what is customary. Litigation issues have been uncharted territory yet Declarant has come up with various successful solutions for some very difficult issues. Declarant has been ever-mindful of the need and desire of all concerned to see the Conservatee progress personally and recover individually, above all else. With that overlay [REDACTED] her as safe an environment as possible to grow, get back on her feet, stabilize her finances, and manage her businesses for growth and stability. The "normal" model for conservator compensation does not fit this conservatorship. Perhaps a close analogy would be decedent's estates of celebrities with marketable assets and business opportunities to develop. Typically, those fiduciaries are really running businesses and are compensated by percentages of income derived, assets under management and additionally for other tasks. Compensating such individuals, and in this case, Declarant [REDACTED] does not properly compensate for the skills, risks, the liabilities, the success and time of those fiduciaries. There is no set compensation in a conservatorship. The Court must take into account the unique circumstances and elements of the particular conservatorship and the benefit of the services realized by the conservatorship. In short, there is no customarily allowed compensation in a conservatorship as unique as this one. The compensation statute provides for reasonable compensation with the court rules as a guide but not a mandate. The "business model", is properly utilized in matters such as this conservatorship.

Declarant has created a stable business environment whereby others have been getting paid millions of dollars. [REDACTED] matters. They all get paid promptly as income is received, without court intervention. Declarant has to manage all of them and the business interests. They work for Declarant and Mr. Spears. Declarant has the oversight for the totality of "Britney Inc.", not just the assets and paying bills. Yet Declarant's compensation has been based upon a model that is not correlated to the scope and the value of his services.

Based upon Declarant's knowledge of the assets, he believes that the entire gross value of the Conservatee's assets, is [REDACTED] Based upon that informed estimate of value as well as the entire scope of Declarant's services, Declarant believes that compensation at the rate [REDACTED] is a reasonable value for Declarant's services. That sum takes into consideration the value of services to manage the business interests in addition to all of the other services outlined herein. Said compensation would be all inclusive, including but not limited to time spent in managing litigation matters. Said amount to be paid in full on a monthly basis.

Jodi Montgomery began working as Britney's care coordinator

in 2018, then became the temporary conservator of her person in 2019. During that period, Ms. Montgomery was paid $95,684.54, plus costs, as reported in the Twelfth Accounting filed in 2020.

Chapter 7

Britney: For the Record

During the first year of the conservatorship, a crew working for MTV chronicled Britney Spears's life and work on the *Circus* album and tour. The authorized documentary was executive produced by her manager, Larry Rudolph. It went behind the scenes and included disagreements, car chases, and poignant interviews with Britney. *Britney: For the Record*, directed by Phil Griffin, premiered on MTV on November 30, 2008.

Although the introduction stated that, "No topic was off limits", the conservatorship was never mentioned. On October 28, 2008, off-camera, Britney's co-conservators filed to make the conservatorships permanent. She did not attend the hearing on the matter.

Filming of *Britney: For the Record* began on September 7, 2008, the day before the live *MTV Video Music Awards* show. The next two months of footage showing Britney's day-to-day life was interspersed with clips from three interviews with Mr. Griffin.

She won three MTV Video Music Awards, recorded the album *Circus*, and was chased by paparazzi. She auditioned dancers and rehearsed choreography. She shot two music videos—*Womanizer* and *Circus*. She took moments to improv new characters to play. She met with record label executives, a perfumer, and the cast of *In the Heights*.

Between it all were stretches of makeup and hair styling and costuming, with conservator father Jamie Spears often nearby to adjust a strap or comment on some shoes. Entertainment managers Mr. Rudolph and Adam Leber frequently dropped into Britney's life, including her home and dressing room. Assistant Brett Miller and security guard Edan Yemini were always at her side.

The conservator/conservatee relationship varied between friendly and contentious. They bickered about Britney keeping her phone. They shared homemade grits. She joked around at his expense. On Halloween, he wore a monster clown costume that made his baby grandsons cry.

While the *Womanizer* video was filmed, Jamie and Randy Phillips, the CEO of AEG Live, chatted about Britney's work regimen. Jamie explained,

> Not any star can do this. We just went in the studio, just playin' around, just to give her somethin' to do. Larry said, "You know we might could do something wi'tha' one." "I don' know, man, we got more important things to do before we worry about an album." It just kinda developed an' everything's gettin' better. All of a sudden, here we are shootin' a video. Y'know— The best thing for her is what she's doin' right now. She's in her element, she's in her world and keepin' her busy. Like, me, I like to go fishin'. She likes to sing an' dance, y'know. And she likes to work.

The interviews offered a revealing glimpse into Britney's state of mind while adjusting to her new lifestyle. She compared the controls on her to the movie *Groundhog Day* and complained that people did not really listen to her.

Talk of her career and celebrity was mixed in with particularly telling statements:

> If I wasn't under the restraints that I am right now, you

know, with all the lawyers and doctors and people analyzing me every day and all that kinda stuff. Like, if that wasn't there, I'd feel so liberated. I'd feel like myself.

You know when you go to jail there's always the time that you know you're gonna get out, you know.

Britney expressed sadness and anger over her situation. During the interviews she always returned to hope and positivity, most intently when talking about her sons:

At this point I have some precious jewels, my two boys, which get me out of bed every morning. I see my babies and I'm like, of course you have to believe in God, you know what I mean? Like I completely believe in God. How could these two be here without there being a God? That'd be heaven for me, to have my kids on an island and a man and no one could get to us.

Chapter 8

Permanent

Eight months after the temporary probate conservatorships over Britney Spears began, Judge Reva Goetz ordered they be made permanent. The hearing for both the estate and person conservatorships took place on October 28, 2008 and the orders were finalized on January 5, 2009.

First, the application and orders for conservatorship of the estate:

Do NOT use this form for a temporary conservatorship.

ATTORNEY Geraldine Wyle, Jeryll Cohen, of Luce, Forward, Hamilton & Scripps LLP

ATTORNEY FOR *(name):* James P. Spears, Co-Conservator of the Estate

FILED Los Angeles Superior Court JAN 05 2009

CONSERVATORSHIP OF *(Name):* Britney Jean Spears CONSERVATEE ORDER APPOINTING PROBATE CONSERVATOR OF THE ESTATE

CASE NUMBER: BP108870

1. The petition for appointment of conservator came on for hearing as follows

a. Judicial officer *(name):* Reva G. Goetz
b. Hearing date: October 28, 2008 Time: 8:30 AM Dept 9

c. Petitioner *(name):* James P. Spears

d. Attorney for petitioner *(name):* James P. Spears

e. Attorney for the conservatee on petition to appoint successor conservator: *(Name):* Samuel D. Ingham, III

f. The person cited was able but unwilling to attend.

THE COURT FINDS

2. All notices required by law have been given.

3. Granting the conservatorship is the least restrictive alternative needed for the protection of the conservatee.

4. *(Name):* Britney Jean Spears b. is substantially unable to manage his or her financial resources or to resist fraud or undue influence,

5. The conservatee a. is an adult.

7. Granting the conservator powers to be exercised independently under Probate Code section 2590 is to the advantage and benefit and in the best interest of the conservatorship estate.

10. Attorney *(name):* Samuel D. Ingham, III has been appointed by the court as legal counsel to represent the conservatee in these proceedings. The cost for representation is: $ See No 21.
The conservatee has the ability to pay all: $

11. The conservatee need not attend the hearing.

12. The appointed court investigator is *(name):* Frank Cowen, Supervising Court Investigator

14. The conservator is a professional fiduciary as defined

by Business and Professions Code section 6501(f). / Co- (Andrew Wallet only)

16. The conservator is not the spouse of the conservatee.

17. The conservator is not the domestic partner or former domestic partner of the conservatee.

THE COURT ORDERS

(Name): Andrew M. Wallet and James P. Spears, as Co-Conservators is appointed conservator of the ESTATE of *(name):* Britney Jean Spears and *Letters of Conservatorship* shall issue upon qualification.

19. The conservatee need not attend the hearing.

20. Bond is fixed at: $ 50,000.00 per conservator to be furnished by an authorized surety company or as otherwise provided by law.

21. For legal services rendered, conservatee's estate shall pay the sum of: $ See terms below.
to *(name):* Samuel D. Ingham, III as follows *(specify terms, including any combination of payors):* The Order previously made with regard to Samuel D. Ingham, III for his services as PVP counsel for the Conservatee, is to remain in full force and effect. (Prior Order: Samuel D. Ingham, III is to receive weekly compensation for legal services rendered on account of no more than $10,000 per week.)

24. The conservator of the estate is granted authorization under Probate Code section 2590 to exercise independently the powers specified in attachment 24 subject to conditions provided.

29. Other orders as specified in attachment 29 are granted.

Judicial officer SIGNATURE FOLLOWS LAST ATTACHMENT

Conservatorship of the Estate of BRITNEY JEAN SPEARS, Conservatee.
LASC Case No. BP108870

ORDER APPOINTING PROBATE CONSERVATOR (ESTATE)
Attachment 24

The Court grants the Co-Conservators the powers pursuant to Probate Code Section 2590 and the following powers set forth in Probate Code Section 2591:

a. To contract for the conservatorship and perform outstanding contracts and thereby bind the estate, including asserting or waiving confidentiality agreements.

b. To operate at the risk of the estate a business constituting an asset of the estate.

c. To pay, collect, compromise, arbitrate, or otherwise adjust claims, debts, or demands upon the Conservatorship Estate.

d. To employ attorneys, accountants, investment counsel, agents, depositaries, and employees and to pay the expenses.

e. To sell Conservatee's residence at public or private sale. Sale may be without confirmation of the Court of this sale, if the purchase price is equal to or exceeds the value of the property as appraised by the Court appointed referee (the "Inventory Value"), or if Mr. Ingham consents to the sale without confirmation of the Court on behalf of the Conservatee; otherwise sale shall be subject to confirmation by the Court.

f. To enter into an exclusive right-to-sell agreement with Tomer Fridman of Ewing & Associates Sotheby's International Realty not to exceed 90 days, for reasonable commission not to exceed 5% of the selling price: and

g. To purchase a replacement residence for the Conservatee.

ORDER APPOINTING PROBATE CONSERVATOR (ESTATE)
Attachment 29

1. The Co-Conservators ("Conservators") of the Estate are granted the following powers in addition to the powers provided by law:

a. The Conservators shall have the power to obtain all documents and records relating to the Conservatee and her assets, whether held in her name or in the name of another, including but not limited to, all records currently in the possession and control of the Conservatee's business manager, Howard Grossman, her attorneys, and others, all contracts, information relating to credit cards, bank statements, estate planning documents, receivables, and any and all powers of attorney.

b. The Conservators shall have the power to take all actions necessary to secure the Conservatee's assets, including the power to enter and take possession and control of the Conservatee's residence, to remove all persons from the residence, and take any and all actions necessary to secure the residence, including changing the locks, call on law enforcement and employ security guards at the expense of the Conservatorship Estate.

c. The Conservators shall have the power to take all actions necessary to secure the Conservatee's liquid assets, including but not limited to, the power to cancel all credit cards.

d. The Conservators shall have the power to revoke all powers of attorneys, including powers of attorney for making health care decisions and managing real estate, and to terminate any and all agencies.

e. The Conservators shall have the power to commence and maintain litigation and participate in any litigation with respect to which the Conservatee is a party or has an interest, and the power to retain counsel and experts, and to pay same from the Conservatorship Estate, not only as to the family law case but for any other matter.

f. The Conservators have the power to perform any and all acts that the Conservatee can perform (whether as an individual or in a representative capacity) with respect to the local, state, or federal tax liabilities of the Conservatee or any entity, trust or foundation in which the Conservatee acts in a representative or ownership capacity (collectively referred to as "Conservatee and related entities"), including but not limited to the power to receive and inspect confidential tax information; receive, and endorse or cash refund checks; sign any and all tax returns, whether income, corporate, employment, partnership, or otherwise; execute a Form 2848 [IRS *Power of Attorney and Declaration of Representative* form]; represent the Conservatee and related entities before all taxing authorities, participate in audits; exercise the rights of the Conservatee and related entities to protest and appeal assessments; pay amounts due to the appropriate taxing authority; execute waivers, tax returns, consents, closing agreements, and similar documents related to the tax liability of the Conservatee and related entities; participate in all procedural matters connected with the tax liability of the Conservatee and related entities; exercise any elections that may be available to the Conservatee and related entities under applicable state or federal tax laws or regulations; to substitute another representative; to request disclosure of tax returns or return information to a third party; and to perform any other acts described in California Probate Code section 4463, except those acts that conflict with or are limited by a more specific provision in this Power.

g. The Conservators have the power to assert the Conservatee's rights in any trust established for her benefit, including but not limited to all revocable inter vivos trusts established by the Conservatee as settlor or trustor, but this power shall not include the power to modify, amend, or revoke any such trusts, without a court order.

h. The Conservators have the power to lease one vehicle

of an appropriate size.[1]

i. The Conservators have the power to prosecute civil harassment restraining orders that they deem to be appropriate.

j. The Conservators have the power and are authorized to pursue opportunities related to professional commitments and activities including but not limited to performing, recording, videos, tours, TV shows, and other similar activities as long as they are approved by Ms. Spears' medical team.

2. The Court grants other Orders as specified below:

a. An inventory and appraisal is to be filed no later than November 21, 2008; and

b. A non-appearance telephonic status hearing is set for November, 21, 2008 at 1:30 P.M. in Department 9 regarding Ms. Spears' professional activities.

APPROVED AS TO FORM AND CONTENT:

Dated: January 5, 2009

//sdi//

Samuel D. Ingham, III

PVP Attorney for Conservatee, Britney Jean Spears

Dated: January 5, 2009

---

[1] Author's note: Based on accounting reports, four vehicles were purchased using estate funds in 2008, including a Yamaha 4-wheeler. In the following years, the conservators also bought a BMW, Cadillac Escalade, and Mercedes Benz; and two ATVs for Britney's niece on her birthday. She also continued paying costs for three vehicles she had purchased for family prior to the conservatorship.

//amw//

Andrew M. Wallet

Co-Conservator of the Estate of Britney Jean Spears

IT IS SO ORDERED.

Dated: Jan 05 2009

//rg//

Hon. Reva Goetz, Judge Pro Tem

Second, the conservatorship application and orders for the conservatorship of the person:

Do NOT use this form for a temporary conservatorship.

Form GC-340 (Rev. July 1, 2008)

ATTORNEY Geraldine Wyle, Jeryll Cohen, of Luce, Forward, Hamilton & Scripps LLP

ATTORNEY FOR *(name):* James P. Spears, Conservator of the Person

FILED

Los Angeles Superior Court JAN 05 2009

CONSERVATORSHIP OF *(Name):* Britney Jean Spears

CONSERVATEE ORDER APPOINTING PROBATE CONSERVATOR OF THE PERSON
CASE NUMBER: BP108870

1. The petition for appointment of conservator came on for hearing as follows

a. Judicial officer *(name):* Reva G. Goetz

b. Hearing date: October 28, 2008 Time: 8:30 AM Dept 9

c. Petitioner *(name):* James P. Spears

d. Attorney for petitioner *(name):* James P. Spears

e. Attorney for the conservatee on petition to appoint successor conservator: *(Name):* Samuel D. Ingham, III

f. The person cited was able but unwilling to attend.

THE COURT FINDS

2. All notices required by law have been given.

3. Granting the conservatorship is the least restrictive alternative needed for the protection of the conservatee.

4. *(Name):* Britney Jean Spears b. is unable properly to provide for his or her needs for physical health, food, clothing, or shelter.

5. The conservatee a. is an adult.

10. Attorney *(name):* Samuel D. Ingham, III has been appointed by the court as legal counsel to represent the conservatee in these proceedings. The cost for representation is: $
The conservatee has the ability to pay all: $

11. The conservatee need not attend the hearing.

12. The appointed court investigator is *(name):*
Frank Cowen

16. The conservator is not the spouse of the conservatee.

17. The conservator is not the domestic partner or former domestic partner of the conservatee.

THE COURT ORDERS

(Name): Andrew M. Wallet and James P. Spears, as Co-Conservators are appointed conservator of the PERSON of *(name):* Britney Jean Spears and *Letters of Conservatorship* shall issue upon qualification.

19. The conservatee need not attend the hearing.

21. For legal services rendered, conservatee's estate shall pay the sum of: $
to *(name):* Samuel D. Ingham, III as follows *(specify terms, including any combination of payors):* The Order previously made with regard to Samuel D. Ingham, III for his services as PVP counsel for the Conservatee, is to remain in full force and effect. (Prior Order: Samuel D. Ingham, III is to receive weekly compensation for legal services rendered on account of no more than $10,000 per week.)

29. Other orders as specified in attachment 29 are granted.

Conservatorship of the Estate of BRITNEY JEAN SPEARS, Conservatee.
LASC Case No. BP108870

ORDER APPOINTING PROBATE CONSERVATOR (PERSON)
Attachment 29

1. The Conservator of the Person is granted the following powers in addition to the powers provided by law:
a. The Conservator shall have the power to restrict and limit visitors by any means, provided that the Conser-

vator shall not prevent the Conservatee from meeting with her court-appointed attorney, Mr. Ingham, except to approve the location for any meetings or visits in advance of any such meetings or visits, and to arrange for appropriate security, in order to protect the Conservatee.

b. The Conservator shall have the power to retain caretakers for the Conservatee on a 24 hour/7 day basis. The power to retain security guards for the Conservatee on a 24 hour/7 day basis.

c. The Conservator shall have the power to prosecute civil harassment restraining orders that the Conservator deems appropriate.

d. The Conservator shall have the power to communicate with treating and other expert medical personnel regarding the Conservatee, and to have access to any and all records (**except psychiatric records**) regarding the Conservatee's medical treatment, diagnosis and testing. The Conservator shall have access, subject to the reasonable discretion of the Conservatee's primary treating psychiatrist located in Los Angeles County, to **any and all records regarding the Conservatee's psychiatric treatment**, diagnosis and testing. [emphasis added]

2. The Court grants other Orders as specified below: The Court appointed 730 expert, Dr. Stephen S. Marmer, M.D., Ph.D., is to remain in place. Further testing is to be conducted as deemed appropriate, necessary, and as directed by Dr. Marmer. The Court's prior sealing orders, regarding HIPAA protected information, remain

in full force and effect, to wit:

(1) all documents that would be protected under the Health Insurance Portability and Accountability Act of 1996 ("HIPAA"), including any and all medical and mental health records that falls within HIPAA, (collectively, "Medical Records") shall be filed under seal;

(2) all pleadings containing confidential information taken from Medical Records or other confidential medical information that falls within HIPAA shall be filed under seal in unredacted form, but shall be publicly filed in redacted form if feasible to do so; and

(3) the courtroom shall be closed whenever there is any discussion or argument concerning confidential information taken from Medical Records or other confidential medical information that falls within HIPAA.

3. It is further ordered that, to the extent that the Conservator wishes to file under seal financial records or to seal the courtroom for proceedings concerning information contained in financial records, he may file a motion to seal pursuant to the procedures and standards set forth in Cal. R. Court 2.550 and 2.551.

APPROVED AS TO FORM AND CONTENT:

Dated: January 5, 2009
//sdi//
Samuel D. Ingham, III
PVP Attorney for Conservatee, Britney Jean Spears

Dated: January 5, 2009
//amw//

Andrew M. Wallet
Co-Conservator of the Estate of Britney Jean Spears

IT IS SO ORDERED.

Dated: Jan 05 2009
//rg//
Hon. Reva Goetz, Judge Pro Tem
Superior Court, State of California

Chapter 9

Mama's Memoir

Through The Storm: A Real Story of Fame and Family in a Tabloid World, co-written by Lorilee Craker and Lynne Spears, was published in September 2008 by Thomas Nelson, an imprint of HarperCollins Christian Publishing. The promotional tour for Lynne's memoir included appearances on the *Today show, Rachael Ray,* and *Larry King Live.* Throughout the book, she repeated that she was not a "stage mom", even preferring to stay in Kentwood, Louisiana over traveling the world with her daughter on a concert tour. Family troubles were often attributed to the vices of her ex-husband, Jamie Spears.

The personal and family history switched to tabloid fodder towards the end. She watched the troubles of her daughter on television from across the country. After Britney's involuntary hospitalization on January 1, 2008, Lynne spent three weeks praying about her before flying to Los Angeles.

On February 1, Lynne filed a statement with Los Angeles Superior Court in support of the conservatorships, the waiver of five-days notice of the conservatorship application, and restraining orders against Sam Lutfi and Adnan Ghalib. That statement was fleshed out and refined in her memoir. There was a clearer narrative of her interactions with Britney and Mr. Lutfi during the week leading up to the conservatorships. She wrote that Mr. Lutfi had repeatedly reached out to her promising a reconciliation. She also alleged that Britney abused drugs and Mr. Lutfi abused Britney.[1]

On the night of January 28, Lou Taylor of Tri Star Sports and Entertainment Group texted Lynne, "GO OVER THERE. THEY HAD A FIGHT." Lynne and friend Jacqueline Butcher rushed to Beverly Hills to try to save Britney. After a security guard got permission to let them through the gate, Jamie "zoomed in" behind Lynne, scaring their daughter away and threatening Mr. Lutfi. Lynne recalled,

> Jamie was stomping, spitting mad, but I could tell he was keeping a tight rein on his emotions. He didn't want to lose control and give Sam the chance to bring charges against him. At one point, he stalked Sam around and around the bar. "You better not be hurting my daughter," he said, over and over again, in a low, menacing voice. "Where is my daughter?"
> (Craker & Spears, 2008)

Lynne wrote that Mr. Lutfi had called her on January 31 with a warning that "somebody was coming to try to commit Britney again." She got to her daughter just in time to witness as "at least twenty police officers stormed into the house." (Craker & Spears, 2008)

Lynne suspected that Mr. Lutfi had called to request the "5150" hold. At the hospital, she saw that "the admittance slip of the psychiatric ward of UCLA Medical Center said [Britney] had been driving recklessly, not taking her medicine as directed, and wasn't sleeping properly. *Aha,* [Lynne] thought. *No one could know that except for Sam."* She conveniently overlooked anyone else who had been in Britney's home as witnesses to such worrisome behavior. Lynne further claimed

---

[1] *See* Chapter 2: Involuntary

she only learned about the conservatorship plans after they went into motion:

> Quiet plans had been underway for six weeks for Jamie to petition the court for temporary conservatorship of Britney. He was going to file for the conservatorship on January 22, eight days beforehand, but he and his business manager, Lou, felt God leading them to wait, fast, and pray, despite the frustration of a phalanx of lawyers.
> (Craker & Spears, 2008)

Ultimately, Lynne was happy for the conservatorships that gave her ex-husband control over their daughter's life and wealth. From Lynne's perspective, the family was on the mend. In a promotional interview with *People* magazine published three weeks after her memoir's release, she said, "The seasons are changing and things are good this year. I am so happy where we are right now." (Dennis, 2008)

Unfortunately for the Spears family, the chapters regarding Mr. Lutfi became the subject of a libel and defamation lawsuit he filed four months after publication.[2]

---

[2] Sam Lutfi vs. Lynne Irene Spears, et al. LASC Case BC 406904. *(See* Chapter 10: Defamation)

Chapter 10

Defamation

On June 30, 2008, Jamie Spears's attorney, Geraldine Wyle, sent Sam Lutfi a letter about no longer pursuing the restraining order against Mr. Lutfi that was filed in February. The letter was included as evidence in a January 30, 2009 temporary restraining order request:

1. Mr. Spears agrees to refrain from pursuit of the existing TRO, and further agrees to take the TRO off calendar.

2. Mr. Lutfi agrees that he will not, in the future, directly contact Britney, purport to take action on Britney's behalf, induce or assist any other person to take or to purport to take action on Britney's behalf, or harass or annoy Britney. Mr. Lutfi further agrees that he will not, in the future, directly or indirectly contact, or harass or annoy Mr. Spears or Lynne Spears.

3. This letter agreement does not affect Mr. Spears' ability to seek a TRO based upon any event occurring on or after July 31, 2008.

4. Nothing herein is intended to be an acknowledgment by Mr. Lutfi that he has committed any of the acts alleged in this matter.

5. This letter agreement and the terms thereof shall be kept strictly confidential. Neither Mr. Spears nor Mr. Lutfi shall directly or indirectly cause to have statements published in any way or in any medium other than that Mr. Lutfi and Mr. Spears have reached a private agreement and that no hearing or order is necessary at this time.

We appreciate your courtesy and cooperation in this matter.

On January 27, 2009, attorney John Anderson sent a letter to Jamie's lawyers about Mr. Lutfi and Jon Eardley leading him to believe that Britney could hire him. Three days later, Jamie filed for a new temporary restraining order against Messrs. Lutfi and Eardley, and Adnan Ghalib.[1]

All three men had to stay at least 250 yards away from and avoid contact with and harassment of not only Britney but her two sons and parents. In addition to standard restraining order limitations, these orders included:

You are prohibited from: (1) acting on Ms. Spears' behalf, or purporting to act on her behalf; (2) inducing or assisting any other person to take action on Ms. Spears' behalf, or to purport to take action on her behalf; and (3) filing, or inducing or assisting any other person to file, legal pleadings that purport to be filed on Ms. Spears' behalf.

Jamie's declaration supporting the need for restraining orders

---

[1] *See* Chapter 3: Representation

alleged harassing text messages and phone calls from Mr. Lutfi to members of Britney's inner circle, as well as attempts to contact Britney herself.

Jamie alleged that on January 10, Mr. Lutfi contacted him via instant messages and phone calls with a combination of threats and offers of help. Jamie referred Mr. Lutfi to his attorney, Blair Berk. Ms. Berk alleged that he then spent weeks texting and calling her regarding meeting with Jamie. Jamie also claimed that Britney had been texting and calling both Messrs. Lutfi and Ghalib.

A "good cause hearing" during which the temporary restraining orders would be adjudged by Judge Aviva Bobb was scheduled for February 23.

On February 3, Mr. Lutfi filed a lawsuit that alleged Jamie had physically attacked him and had not paid him for services performed while working as Britney's manager. He also accused Lynne Spears of libel against him in her memoir (Craker & Spears, 2008).[2]

The complaint contended that Jamie and Lynne were focused on controlling Britney and her fortune; the Spears publicly blamed Mr. Lutfi for Britney's troubles and used her vulnerable state as an opportunity to conserve her:

> Seeing Lutfi's involvement with Britney as a threat to their lifestyle, Jamie and Lynne launched a campaign of lies and intimidation designed to destroy Lutfi and drive him out of Britney's life. This campaign also provided Jamie with the opportunity he needed to obtain an appointment as Britney's conservator (for which he receives a reported $16,000 per month in compensation).

---

[2] *See* Chapter 9: Mama's Memoir

Although, still deemed "incompetent", Britney has recently recorded a new album, "Circus", embarked on a world tour and given numerous media interviews and continues to earn the money that supports Jamie's and Lynne's lavish lifestyle. Despite seemingly accomplishing their objectives, Jamie and Lynne have nevertheless continued their smear campaign against Lutfi. Thus, having no other alternative, Lutfi brings this action to defend himself against Jamie's and Lynne's persistent attacks.

The suit included quotes about Mr. Lutfi from Lynne's memoir. There was also a recounting of an alleged altercation during which Jamie physically assaulted and threatened Mr. Lutfi at Britney's home. He claimed that Jamie's and Lynne's behavior caused physical and emotional harm to him, as well as a loss of reputation that made it hard to find a job.

In June, he filed statements from four people who had been in Britney's life before the conservatorship began to directly refute Lynne's accusations.

First, Adnan Ghalib, a paparazzo and Britney's former boyfriend:

On January 3, 2008, while I was at home watching television, I heard a report stating that Britney had been transported to Cedars-Sinai Medical Center, via ambulance, and placed on a seventy-two (72) hour psychiatric evaluation.

On January 4, 2008, I received a telephone call and several text messages from Britney requesting that I visit her at Cedars-Sinai. That evening, I went to the hospital and visited with Britney.

Shortly after the January 3, 2008 incident, it became public knowledge that I was dating Britney. Consequently, I was contacted by numerous television shows, entertainment magazines and other media with requests for interviews about Britney and the events leading up to her being taken to Cedars-Sinai.

I was initially reluctant to give any interviews and refused to do so. However, a week or so after the January 3, 2008 incident, I received a telephone call from Britney's mother, Lynne Spears ("Lynne"), wherein she instructed me to give an interview and tell the interviewer that everything was fine with Britney; that Britney was not on drugs or an alcoholic; and that all of Britney's problems including, without limitation, accusations of drug abuse, erratic behavior, etc., were caused by Lutfi.

On or about January 22, 2008, per Lynne's instruction, I gave the interview, however, I did not blame Britney's problems on Lutfi, as Lynne instructed, because I had no personal knowledge, or any reason to believe, that any of Lynne's accusations or assertions about Lutfi were true.

I am informed and believe that Lynne has stated on page 176 of her book, "Through the Storm", that I told her that Lutfi hid Britney's cell phones and then told Britney that he (Lutfi) lost them. Lynne's statement is false. At no time did I ever tell Lynne that Lutfi hid Britney's cell phones or that Lutfi told Britney that he (Lutfi) had lost them.

I am informed and believe that, in her book, "Through the Storm", Lynne asserts that Lutfi told her that he had cut the phone lines at Britney's house. Based on my own personal knowledge and experience, I do not believe that this assertion is true.

First, at all times when I lived at the house, the telephones at Britney's house were always in working order. In addition, there is a fax machine in a small office in the house that was always working. I often used the fax telephone to make calls when other phone lines were in use or unavailable.

Second, the complex in which the house is located is a gated community guarded by a security guard located at the front gate entrance. The guard only allows visitors into the complex after receiving approval from the residents of the complex. In order to obtain approval for Britney's visitors, the guard has to call Britney's house on the telephone. Had the phone lines been cut, as alleged, security would have been unable to communicate with anyone in the house and, consequently, visitors, including Lynne, would not have been able to enter the complex.

Third, Britney's house is also gated. The gate is controlled by a keypad that is connected to Britney's house via the phone lines. Had the phone lines been cut, as alleged, visitors, including Lynne, would not have been able to communicate with anyone in the house and would not have been able to enter the property.

Second, Alli Sims, Britney's cousin and live-in personal assistant:

> I lived with Britney in her Beverly Hills, California and Malibu, California homes during the period of February 2007 through October 2007. After October 2007, although I no longer lived with Britney, I was in contact with her nearly every day.

> I acted as a de-facto personal assistant to Britney during the period of March 2007 through August 2007.

> I am informed and believe that Britney's mother, Lynne Spears ("Lynne") has stated in her book, "Through the Storm", that she believed that Sam Lutfi ("Lutfi") was intentionally trying to shut Britney's family out of her life. Based on my own personal knowledge and experience, I do not believe that Lynne's belief has any valid foundation.

> During the period I lived with Britney and served as her personal assistant, and during the months that followed, I was in constant contact with Lutfi and spoke with him nearly every day.

> At no time during the period I lived with Britney and served as her personal assistant, or during the months that followed, did I ever hear Lutfi say anything negative about Britney's parents. In fact, I often heard Lutfi encouraging Britney to make amends with her

parents and invite them back into her life. For her part, Britney was resistant to Lutfi's suggestions and wanted nothing to do with her parents whom she believed had betrayed her.

I am also informed and believe that, in her book, Lynne asserts that Lutfi told her that he threw away all of Britney's cell phone chargers and cut phone lines at Britney's house. Based on my own personal knowledge and experience, I do not believe that this assertion is true.

During the period I lived with Britney and served as her personal assistant, and during the months that followed, there was a large cell phone docking station located on one of the tables in Britney's house. On numerous occasions, I witnessed the docking station being used to charge multiple cell phones, including Britney's.

During the period I lived with Britney and served as her personal assistant, and during the months that followed, I often received telephone calls from Britney from her cell phone. I also witnessed Britney making and receiving calls on her cell phone on nearly a daily basis.

At no time during the period I lived with Britney and served as her personal assistant, or during the months that followed, did I ever witness Britney without a working cell phone. In fact, I witnessed Britney making and receiving calls on her cell phone on nearly a daily basis.

At no time during the period I lived with Britney and

served as her personal assistant, or during the months that followed, did Britney ever mention being unable to make calls from her cell phone or any other phone in her house.

At no time during the period I lived with Britney and served as her personal assistant, or during the months that followed did I ever experience difficulty making telephone calls from any of her house phones, nor did I ever have trouble reaching Britney on the house phones.

Next, Robin Johnson, who oversaw Britney's visits with her children:

I have worked as a Supervised Visitation Monitor for about 10 years. For all times relevant hereto, I have been, and remain, the Owner of Family Care Monitoring Services, a California corporation in good standing. As a family care monitor, I am often retained by attorneys in high-profile celebrity cases to monitor, witness and report on a subject celebrity's behavior and interaction with children and other family members. My reports are often used as evidence in child custody and marriage dissolution proceedings.

In or about October 2007, Family Care Monitoring Services was retained by the law firm of Trope & Trope, attorneys for Britney Spears ("Britney"), to monitor, witness and report on Britney's interaction with her two children [REDACTED]. I was the primary monitor assigned to the case. There were two alternate monitors.

For all but one week during a seven (7) month period of October 2007 through April 2008, I monitored Britney and her children each week from approximately noon on Friday through the following Monday morning, and on Tuesdays from approximately 9:00 a.m. to approximately 5:00 p.m. During that seven month time period, my sole responsibility was to monitor and document how Britney behaved and interacted with her two children.

For most of the time I was with Britney, the only persons constantly present with her were the two children, a housekeeper named Sabi, and one of three of Britney's personal assistants, including, without limitation, her cousin, Alli Sims.

Sam Lutfi ("Lutfi") was also present approximately two-thirds of the time I was monitoring Britney. Lutfi never slept over at Britney's home in Malibu, California at any time when I was present. Mr. Lutfi often spent the night in a guest room at Britney's home in Beverly Hills. My room was located between Lutfi's and Britney's rooms.

I am informed and believe that Britney's mother, Lynne Spears ("Lynne") has stated in her book, "Through the Storm", that she believed Mr. Lutfi was intentionally trying to shut Britney's family out of her life. Based on my own personal knowledge and experience, I do not believe that Lynne's belief has any valid foundation.

During the time I monitored Britney, Lutfi constantly encouraged Britney to make peace with her parents, especially her mother, Lynne. For example, on more than one occasion, Lynne would call or send Britney a text message. Britney would then get irate, yelling and calling her mother names. On each of these occasions, Lutfi would attempt to calm Britney down and would encourage her to call Lynne or respond to the message.

On one occasion, in November 2007, I was present at Britney's residence when Lynne appeared at the front gate asking to be let in. I witnessed Britney refuse to allow her mother to enter. I also witnessed Lutfi telling Britney that she should let Lynne into the house to talk.

I am also informed and believe that, in her book, Lynne asserts that Lutfi told her that he had thrown away all of Britney's cell phone chargers and cut phone lines at Britney's house. Based on my own personal knowledge and experience, I do not believe that this assertion is true.

At all times during the period in which I monitored Britney, the telephones at her houses were always in order. I was keenly aware of this fact since, as a family care monitor, I must have the ability to make emergency telephone calls at all times. Since cell phone reception is very poor around Britney's homes, my ability to use house telephones was a necessity.

On several occasions, I witnessed Britney calling the telephone company and requesting that her telephone service be disconnected or asking her housekeeper, Sabi, to make such a call. In addition, based on the fact that I often saw Britney talking on her cell phones, I do not believe there was ever any time in which Lutfi confiscated any or all of Britney's cell phone chargers.

I am informed and believe that, in her book, Lynne also asserts that Lutfi told her that he had ground up pills, such as [REDACTED], in Britney's food in attempt to keep her sedated and out of trouble. Based on my own personal knowledge and experience, I do not believe that this assertion is true. As a family care monitor, I am required to be aware of all drugs (prescription or otherwise) being taken by the persons I am monitoring. During the seven month period in which I monitored Britney, she was taking [REDACTED] as prescribed by her doctors. I witnessed Britney taking this medication on an almost daily basis. I am unaware that she had been prescribed any other such medications. I also witnessed that the [REDACTED] had the opposite of a sedating effect on Britney.

Finally, Filipe Teixeira, a paparazzo:

I had followed Britney to a Ralph's grocery. While I was waiting outside, I received a telephone call from Britney asking me to join her inside. Shortly thereafter, Britney and I left the grocery store in my car. While we were driving, Britney grew concerned about leaving her car in the grocery store parking lot. She then had me drive her back to the store to pick up her car. Britney and I left the store in our separate cars and returned to her home in Beverly Hills. When we arrived at the Beverly Hills residence, Lutfi was there. Lutfi appeared happy to see Britney and she appeared happy to see him. We then went inside the house and ordered food.

Around 7:00 p.m. that same night, Britney received news that her father had arrived. Britney stated that she did not want to see him. Britney then got in her car and asked me to come with her. While in her car, Britney repeatedly stated that she was afraid of her father and did not want to see him. While I was still in the car, and before we had gone too far, Adnan Ghalib, another paparazzo, arrived and blocked Britney's car with his own, causing her to stop. Britney initially seemed startled by Mr. Ghalib's actions, but subsequently got into Mr. Ghalib's car and left.

I returned Britney's car to the Beverly Hills residence around 9:00 p.m. When I arrived, Lutfi was at the residence along with Britney's mother, Lynne Spears ("Lynne") and her friend, "Jackie". During the ensuing half hour, I witnessed Lutfi repeatedly trying to convince Lynne to go after her daughter. While in my presence, Lynne, while expressing concern over her daughter's whereabouts, refused to do so, stating that she did not want to have to deal with the paparazzi. Lynne Spears appeared more concerned about herself than she did about her daughter, Britney. Shortly thereafter, I overheard Lutfi calling Mr. Ghalib and asking him to bring Britney back to the Beverly Hills residence. I left the residence shortly after Britney returned.

I am informed and believe that, in her book, Lynne asserts that Lutfi told her that he disabled Britney's cars so that she could not leave her house unattended. Based on my own personal knowledge and experience, I do not believe that this assertion is true. Throughout the period I was with Britney, I often witnessed her driving her cars and often at dangerous speeds, well in excess of the legal speed limit. In fact, on one occasion, I was pulled over for speeding while attempting to keep up with and follow Britney. On one particular occasion, I heard Britney's doctor advise Lutfi that it would not be a good idea for Britney to be allowed to drive as a result of her being on medication and her medical condition.

At no time during the period in which I worked with Britney did I ever witness Britney have any difficulty starting any of her cars. In fact, in all of the time Britney and I were together, neither Britney nor I had any difficulty starting any of her cars.

Mr. Lutfi subpoenaed depositions from Britney, Jamie, and Lynne. When the conservators inevitably pushed back against Britney testifying, he requested a third-party medical evaluator to determine whether she genuinely lacked capacity to testify.

He also requested documents as evidence to disprove Lynne's accusations of drug abuse:

Any and all DOCUMENTS which you identify, or should identify, in your responses to the form interrogatories served concurrently herewith.

Any and all DRUG TEST REPORTS concerning tests of

Britney Spears taken during the period October 1, 2007 through March 1, 2008.

Any and all BABY MONITOR REPORTS concerning Britney Spears and/or her children, pertaining to any period between October 1, 2007 and March 1, 2008.

Unfortunately, Mr. Lutfi also accused Britney of drug abuse during the period when he worked as her manager in his motion to compel Jamie to produce documents on March 31, 2011. He claimed that he "did everything [he] could to *discourage* Britney from taking drugs." [emphasis supplied] He claimed he "got her completely off drugs, and her drug tests all came back 'clean.'" He insisted that after he cleaned her up, the only drugs she took during that period were prescription medications.

Through a few years of back and forth about evidence discovery, Jamie, Lynne, and Mr. Lutfi eventually sat for depositions, but not Britney. The initial case stretched out until a judgment against Mr. Lutfi was made on November 28, 2012 because he hadn't proven his allegations. On December 31, 2012, he filed with The Court of Appeal of the State of California, 2nd Appellate District, Division 2 (Case No. B246253). Once the case was in front of different judges, it was determined that the probate court did not have the power to prevent a witness from testifying in another unrelated matter without making its own findings regarding the witness's ability to testify.

On May 3, 2016, Britney finally testified in a deposition and did not have worsened mental health problems as her conservators speculated could happen in their oppositions to Mr. Lutfi's subpoenas. (Kovaleski & Coscarelli, 2016) On September 9, 2016, the Spears's and Mr. Lutfi reached a private settlement in the case that was billed to Britney's estate.

Chapter 11

You Better Work

In October 2008, Judge Reva Goetz ordered the conservatorships over Britney Spears be made permanent due to her grave disabilities. Over the next decade the churn continued with more albums, live performances, TV appearances, and music videos. Below is an incomplete list of her labors.

2009

March
- *The Circus Starring Britney Spears Tour*
  March 3, 2009-November 29, 2009
  97 concerts across the United States, Canada, England, Ireland, France, Belgium, Denmark, Sweden, Finland, Russia, Germany, and Australia.
- "If You Seek Amy" music video

June
- *New Now Next Awards*

July
- "Radar" music video
- "Kill the Lights" music video

August
- *The Teen Choice Awards* TV special

- *The Late Show with David Letterman* episode "Episode #16.189"

September
- *MTV Video Music Awards* live TV special

October
- "3" music video

November
- *The Circus Starring Britney Spears* international tour end

December
- *Billboard's New Year's Eve Live* TV special

2010

January
- *The 52nd Annual Grammy Awards* live TV special

August
- "Radiance" perfume commercial

September
- *Glee* episode "Britney/Brittany"

2011

February
- "Hold It Against Me" music video
- *Good Morning America* TV magazine

March
- *Good Morning America* TV magazine

- *Jimmy Kimmel Live!* episode "#9.102"
- *The Ellen DeGeneres Show* episode #8.130
- *Femme Fatale* album

April
- "Till the World Ends" music video
- *Nickelodeon's Kids Choice Awards* TV special
- *Britney Spears: I Am the Femme Fatale* TV special

May
- *Jimmy Kimmel Live!* episode "#9.134"
- "Wango Tango" concert guest host
- *The 2011 Billboard Music Awards* TV Special

June
- "I Wanna Go" music video
- *Femme Fatale Tour*
  June 16, 2011-December 10, 2011
  79 concerts across the United States, Canada, Russia, Ukraine, Hungary, Croatia, Switzerland, France, Belgium, Denmark, Sweden, Finland, Germany, Netherlands, Ireland, Northern Ireland, England, Portugal, United Arab Emirates, Brazil, Argentina, Chile, Peru, Colombia, Venezuela, Mexico, Dominican Republic, and Puerto Rico.

August
- *MTV Video Music Awards* live TV special

October
- "Criminal" music video
- "The X Factor Digital Experience"

November
- *Britney Spears Live: The Femme Fatale Tour* documentary

December
- *Femme Fatale Tour* end

2012

June
- *The Pauly D Project* episode "Divas, Diamonds and D****"

July
- *Teen Choice Awards* TV special

September
- *The X Factor* season 2 premiere
- *Jimmy Kimmel Live!* episode "#10.242"
- *The Ellen DeGeneres Show* episode #10.2

October
- *iHeartRadio Music Festival* TV special
- *The Tonight Show with Jay Leno* episode "#21.26"

November
- "Fantasy Twist" perfume commercial
- "Scream & Shout" music video

December
- *The X Factor* season 2 finale

2013

July
- "Ooh La La" music video

September
- *Good Morning America* TV magazine

October
- *iHeartRadio Music Festival* TV special
- "Work Bitch" music video
- *Miley: The Movement* documentary

November
- *The Ellen DeGeneres Show* episode #11.62
- *Britney Jean* album

December
- "Perfume" music video
- *I Am Britney Jean* documentary
- *The Ellen DeGeneres Show* episode #11.68
- *Britney: Piece of Me* residency
  December 27, 2013-December 27, 2017
  248 concerts in Las Vegas

2014

January
- *The 40th Annual People's Choice Awards* TV special

May
- *Billboard Music Awards* TV special

September
- *The Tonight Show Starring Jimmy Fallon* episode "Keith Richards/Debra Messing/The Replacements"
- *Good Morning America* TV magazine

November
- *Jimmy Kimmel Live!* episode "#12.160"

2015

January
- *Super Bowl 2015* commercial

February
- *Jimmy Kimmel Live!* episode "#13.16"

May
- "Pretty Girls" music video
- *Billboard Music Awards* TV special
- *The Ellen DeGeneres Show* episode #12.150

July
- *The 2015 ESPY Awards* TV special

August
- *Teen Choice Awards* TV special
- *MTV Video Music Awards* live TV special

November
- *Jane the Virgin* episode "Chapter Twenty-Seven"
- *Restore the Shore* fundraiser TV special

2016

May
- "Britney Spears American Dream" video game
- *Billboard Music Awards* TV special

June
- *Jamie Lynn Spears: When the Lights Go Out* documentary
- "Make Me" music video

July
- "Private Show" perfume commercial

August
- *Jimmy Kimmel Live!* episode "#14.104"
- *The Late Late Show with James Corden* "Carpool Karaoke"
- *MTV Video Music Awards* live TV special
- *Glory* album
- "Make Me..." music video

September
- *The Ellen DeGeneres Show* episode #14.2
- iHeartRadio Music Festival
- Apple Music Festival

October
- *The Jonathan Ross Show* season 11 episode 4

November
- "Slumber Party" music video

December
- KIIS-FM Jingle Ball

- 99.7 NOW's Triple Ho Show
- B96 Jingle Bash
- *Dick Clark's New Year's Rockin' Eve* live TV special

2017

April
- *Radio Disney Music Awards* TV special

June
- *Britney: Live in Concert Tour*
  June 3, 2017- July 3, 2017
  11 concerts across Japan, South Korea, Taiwan, Philippines, Thailand, Hong Kong, Singapore, and Israel.

July
- *Britney: Live in Concert Tour* end

December
- *Britney: Piece of Me* residency end

2018

April
- 29th Annual GLAAD Media Awards

July
- "My Prerogative" perfume commercial
- *Piece of Me Tour*
  July 12, 2018-October 21, 2018
  31 concerts across the United States, England, Germany, Denmark, Norway, Sweden, Belgium,

Ireland, Scotland, and France.

August
- "Apple Music" commercial

October
- *United States Grand Prix*
- *Piece of Me Tour* end
- *The Ellen DeGeneres Show* episode #16.29

2019

September
- *Corporate Animals* movie

Chapter 12

Residency

Throughout the four months leading up to the opening of Britney Spears's first Las Vegas residency, a crew working for World of Wonder Productions chronicled her life and work preparing for the live shows. Executive producers of the authorized documentary included Britney and her managers Adam Leber and Larry Rudolph. *I Am Britney Jean*, directed by Fenton Bailey and Randy Barato, was billed as an intimate look at Britney and released on E! on December 22, 2013.

The running theme of the movie was that the opening night deadline was too close. Whoever set it did not understand how much labor and time went into such a large-scale production. Filming of the movie began in early September 2013, 114 days before the first concert of the *Britney: Piece of Me* series began. An onscreen countdown punctuated scenes throughout the documentary, keeping the looming deadline at top of mind. The theatre at Planet Hollywood Las Vegas Resort & Casino needed to be gutted and reconstructed. Dancers needed to be hired and trained. Large props and scenery needed to be constructed. Hundreds of costumes needed to be fashioned. And Britney needed to squeeze time for residency preparation into her already packed schedule.

Her new album, *Britney Jean,* was still undergoing finishing touches in advance of its November 29 release. She also needed to promote two singles, the full album, and the residency. Much of the on-camera promotion featured nervous hand-wringing and insistences that she was shy.

She was shown attending some early creative meetings, the final round of dancer auditions, and one early costume fitting. The countdown on pre-production labors weighed on the residency crew. While Britney was working photo shoots and music videos, Show Director Baz Halpin was figuring out how to create a giant rotating tree. While Britney took a brief trip to London to call out "Work Bitch" while waving a whip on TV programs, dancers in Los Angeles were puking from exhaustion in the push to learn all their choreography in one month.

In mid-November, an emergency scheduling meeting came together to hammer out details on when Britney could be available for which tasks. The meeting included Mr. Halpin, AD Melissa Garcia, dad Jamie Spears, managers Messrs. Leber and Rudolph, day-to-day manager Florence Tse, and business management Robin Greenhill. They had to juggle rehearsals (in California and Nevada), TV appearances, and video shoots. Lastly came personal days. Jamie planned to care for Britney's two sons, which kept him from wandering about on sets. When the subject of December 2 arose, people remarked that it was both Britney's birthday and when she was scheduled to appear on *The Ellen DeGeneres Show.*

When Mr. Halpin asked if Britney could rehearse on her birthday, Ms. Greenhill cheerfully replied, "Sure. What do you want her to play?"

He clarified that he needed rehearsal time with Britney and Ms. Greenhill confirmed, "She's gonna rehearse it."

Ms. Greenhill's role was part of the unusual conservatorship arrangement. She worked for Lou Taylor at Tri Star Sports and Entertainment Group, which managed the books for Britney's estate. Yet as "business management", Ms. Greenhill wielded control over the conservatee's schedule, shadowed her, and occasionally acted as personal assistant.

On Britney's birthday, she chatted with Ellen DeGeneres backstage before her eponymous talk show began. Ellen remarked on Britney working on her birthday. Surrounded by managers, she insisted, "I love working on my birthday. It's okay. I love work. It's fun. If I'm not working, I'd be, like, getting into something. Like, I don't know what to do with myself."

Rather than an intimate look at who Britney really was, most of her screen time was interview clips of pleasantries. She believed in a higher power. She liked sex. She had inspirational quotes in her bathroom:

> There's a saying that I have in my bathroom in Louisiana. "Go beyond reason to love for it's the only safety there is." And it's true. You should always go beyond reason to love and to be with the person that you want to be with and to be cherished and to be treasured. I think it's why we're here as people.

Through it all, whenever Britney noticed a camera was on her she lit up and made friendly conversation. But her manager Mr. Rudolph had to make sure that everyone knew how shy she was as a child:

> ... incredibly down to Earth and incredibly down home. She really was the girl next door. You know that sweet little Southern girl next door. That's really who she is. She really hasn't changed from that core in all these years. And when she's off that stage and she's not being Britney Spears, that's who she is. She's just a little girl from Kentwood, Louisiana.

The documentary finished with the song "Stronger" over a montage of elite dancers rehearsing on the Planet Hollywood stage . . . Then a final counter for the impending deadline.

The *Britney: Piece of Me* residency opened on December 27, 2013. The concert series was originally contracted for two years and was extended twice. The final performance was New Year's Eve 2017. The 248 concerts were estimated to have grossed over $130 million.

During summer 2017, Britney did a one month international tour in between Las Vegas residency concerts. From June 3 to July 7, 2017, she performed a total of 11 concerts across Japan, South Korea, Taiwan, Philippines, Thailand, Hong Kong, Singapore, and Israel. The tour was estimated to have grossed over $16 million.

She recalled that her management forced her to sign on for the 2018 *Piece of Me Tour* in a court statement on June 23, 2021 at a hearing on her conservatorship case:

> My management said if I don't do this tour, I will have to find an attorney, and by contract, my own management could sue me if I didn't follow through with the tour. He handed me a sheet of paper as I got off the stage in Vegas and said I had to sign it. It was very threatening and scary. And with the conservatorship, I couldn't even get my own attorney. So out of fear, I went ahead and I did the tour.

Britney had a half-year break from performing, then began the *Piece of Me Tour* on July 12, 2018. She performed 31 concerts across the United States, England, Germany, Denmark, Norway, Sweden, Belgium, Ireland, Scotland, and France. The tour wrapped up in Texas on October 21, 2018 and was estimated to have grossed $54 million.

Chapter 13

Break

In the era of online music streaming, live concerts were known to increasingly bring in more money than music sales. Each year, *Billboard* magazine released estimates of revenue from touring and music sales of the top highest-paid musicians. In 2018, among the top ten earners, the average touring revenue was 85% of their total revenue for the year. (Billboard, 2018) According to *Statista,* between 2008 and 2018, sales of both physical and digital music decreased by almost 60%. (Götting, 2023) In 2018, Britney's management team decided to break away from the pattern of alternating a tour with an album.

The night before the final *Piece of Me* concert, Britney attended a flashy outdoor event in Las Vegas to announce another residency. *Britney: Domination* was scheduled to run from February 13 to August 17, 2019 at the Park MGM. (Legaspi, 2018) Tickets went on sale the next week, on October 26. Dancer auditions began two weeks after that. Dance rehearsal videos started popping up on social media in mid-December.

Britney recalled the period in a hearing on the conservatorship on June 23, 2021:

> I started rehearsing early, but it was hard because I'd been doing Vegas for four years, and I needed a break in between. But, no, I was told this is the timeline and this is how it's gonna go. I rehearsed four to four [sic] days a week. I was basically directing most of the show. I

taught my dancers my new choreography myself. I take everything I do very seriously. There are tons of videos with me at the rehearsals. I wasn't good; I was great.

I led a room of 16 new dancers in rehearsals. It's funny to hear my managers' side of the story. They all said I wasn't participating in rehearsals, and I never agreed to take my medication, which my medication is only taken in the mornings, never at rehearsal. They don't even see me, so why are they even claiming that? When I said no to one dance move into rehearsals, it was as if I planted a huge bomb somewhere, and I said, "No. I don't want to do it this way."

After that, my management, and my dancers, and my assistant of the new people that were supposed to do the new show all went into a room, shut the door, and didn't come out for at least 45 minutes.

I was told by my, at the time therapist, Dr. [Timothy] Benson, who died, that my manager called at that moment and told him I wasn't cooperating or following the guidelines in rehearsals, and he also said I wasn't taking my medication, which is so dumb because I've had the same lady every morning for the past eight years giving me my same medication, and I'm nowhere near these stupid people. It made no sense at all.

There was a week period where they were nice to me. They said if I don't wanna do the new Vegas show, I don't have to, because I was getting really nervous. I said, "I can wait." It was like lifting literally 200 pounds off of me when she said I don't have to do the show anymore because it was really, really hard on myself and it was too much. I couldn't take it anymore. So I remember telling my assistant that, "But you know what? I feel weird if I say, 'No.' I feel like they're gonna come back and be mean to me or punish me or something."

Several weeks into ticket sales for the upcoming residency, Britney's management team decided to cancel the whole run of concerts. However, arguing about choreography was not a legitimate excuse for scrapping such a large production.
In her June 2021 courtroom statement, Britney continued,

Three days later after I said, *No* to Vegas, my therapist sat me down in a room and said he had a million phone calls about how I was not cooperating in rehearsals, and I haven't been taking my medication. All of this was false.

He immediately, the next day, put me on lithium out of nowhere. He took me off my normal meds I've been on five years and lithium is a very, very strong and completely different medication compared to what I was used to. He put me on that and I felt drunk. I really couldn't even take up for myself. I couldn't even have a conversation with my mom or dad, really, about anything. I told him I was scared and my doctor had me on—six different nurses with this new medication, come to my home, stay with me to monitor me on this new medication which I never wanted to be on to begin with.

Anything that happened to me had to be approved by

my dad, and my dad only—he acted like he didn't know that I was told I had to be tested over the Christmas holidays, before they sent me away, when my kids went home to Louisiana. He was the one who approved all of it. My whole family did nothing.

Over the two-week holiday, a lady came into my home for four hours a day, sat me down, and did a psych test on me. It took forever. . . I was told I had to.

On Instagram, she described another round of tests during that period, referring to the facility she was checked into in early 2019 as "that place":

I had three MRIs before I went to that place. I wasn't complaining about anything. I was just told I had to go. It was my dad and I had no rights at the time.

So I did it and I was immediately like, *Why am I having to go to do these MRIs so many times?* Because when I was younger, I had a cyst on my chest when I was like eight years old. They did an MRI, because they thought it was cancer, but it wasn't, it was completely fine. So whenever I hear the word MRI, I kind of was like, *Oh, that's a big deal. Like, something must be wrong with me.*

But I remember when I was younger, and I was like eight, and I stayed in that machine for no more than 30 minutes. You had to do it all over again if you moved.

But when I went during the conservatorship right before they sent me to that place, I did it three times. And I stayed in there for an hour each time, which is a lot of

being still and had to go back three times.
@britneyspears (2022, September 11)

Between the two weeks of psychological evaluation and three hours of MRI scans, Britney's mental and physical health had been thoroughly documented. However, when the residency cancelation was announced on January 4, 2019, dad Jamie Spears's poor health was to blame.

A post on Britney's Instagram account explained,

> I don't even know where to start with this, because this is so tough for me to say. I will not be performing my new show Domination. I've been looking forward to this show and seeing all of you this year, so doing this breaks my heart. However, it's important to always put family first... and that's the decision I had to make. A couple months ago, my father was hospitalized and almost died. We're all so grateful that he came out of it alive, but he still has a long road ahead of him. I had to make the difficult decision to put my full focus and energy on my family at this time. I hope you all can understand. More information on ticket refunds is available on britneyspears.com. I appreciate your prayers and support for my family during this time. Thank you, and love you all... always.

@britneyspears (2019, January 4).

The multitude of expensive problems caused by canceling the series of concerts just six weeks before opening night implied the severity of Jamie's medical condition.

Later that day, *Billboard* reported on the cancelation:

Sources say the cancelation could cost Spears her guarantee for the show, which could be worth several million dollars. There would also be costs for the venue and its owners MGM Grand, which likely already invested in preproduction for the show.

While it's unclear whether Spears' insurance would cover lost revenue, Paul Bassman of Ascend Insurance, which services the live entertainment industry, says it's common for artists to have policies that cover cancelation due to a family member's illness. But typically those policies only cover life-threatening illnesses. "Since her father is expected to recover, that's typically not something that would be covered," Bassman says, adding that he does not have any inside knowledge of Spears' policy for the show.
(Brooks, 2019)

Just three days later, photos were published showing Britney enjoying her break. She was driving herself and her boyfriend to In-N-Out to pick up burgers. (Vacco-Bolanos, 2019) Lit by California sunshine, she did not look distraught over a family member's serious illness. The respite from the churn of her career did not last long.

Britney recalled in her June 2021 court statement,

> I got a phone call from my dad saying, after I did this psych test with this lady, basically saying I had failed the test. "I'm sorry, Britney. You have to listen to your doctors. They are planning to send you to a small home in Beverly Hills to do a small rehab program that we're going to make up for you. You're going to pay $60,000 a

month for this."

I cried on the phone for an hour, and he loved every minute of it. The control he had over someone as powerful as me. As he loved the control to hurt his own daughter 100,000 percent. He loved it.

I packed my bags and went to that place. I worked seven days a week, no days off, which in California the only similar thing to this is called sex trafficking, making anyone work, work against their will, taking all their possessions away; credit cards, cash, phone, passport, car, and placing them in the home where they work with the people who live with them. They all lived in the house with me, the nurses, the 24/7 security. They watched me change every day, naked, morning, noon, and night.

I had no privacy door for my room. I gave eight [vials] of blood a week. If I didn't do any of my meetings—and worked [with therapists] from 8:00 to 6:00 at night, which is 10 hours a day, 7 days a week, no days off—I wouldn't be able to see my kids or my boyfriend. I never had a say in my schedule. They always told me I had to do this . . . I wouldn't be able to see my kids or my boyfriend.

Since lithium levels need to be closely monitored, her blood was drawn for testing several times a week. In her July 2021 court statement, she recalled, "When they drew blood, I would have to use three different needles sometimes to get the right vein, and I didn't want to give blood or be on lithium."

Reflecting on her experience in that July 2021 statement,

she said, "And there's a million-dollar question. Why would they do that? I have no idea. So honestly I started honestly just to think they were trying to kill me."

In February 2019, Jamie was in Nashville finalizing his plans to become the sole conservator of both Britney's estate and person. On March 4, co-conservator of the estate Andrew Wallet broke away from the case in an urgent resignation to Judge Brenda Penny at Los Angeles Superior Court.

In his petition to Judge Penny, Britney's court-appointed attorney Samuel Ingham insisted,

> The conservatorship is engaged in numerous ongoing business activities requiring immediate attention and it therefore is in the best interest of the conservatee that the acceptance of WALLET'S resignation and the issuance of amended letters of conservatorship of the estate occur immediately and without delay. <u>Substantial detriment, irreparable harm and immediate danger will result to the conservatee and her estate if the relief requested herein is not granted on an ex parte basis.</u> [emphasis supplied]

On top of the torturous combination of daily interrogation, forced nudity, sedation, and isolation from loved ones, Britney also didn't know when the program made up for her would end, as she recalled in her July 2021 statement:

> They also never let me know when I could leave. My dad called the jerk at that place and I asked him, "Can you please tell them to let me go home?" And he said, "Something must be wrong with you if you want to know when you get to go home."

On April 3, the first Instagram post on Britney's profile since the January 4 cancelation message featured an image of the words, "Fall in love with taking care of yourself. Mind. Body. Spirit." The accompanying caption read, "We all need to take time for a little 'me time' :)" (@britneyspears, 2019, April 3) Later that month, Britney began getting some time out of the facility she was being held in—occasionally popping up around Los Angeles.

On April 16, 2019, the podcast *Britney's Gram* released an episode featuring a voicemail message from someone purporting to have worked at one of the various law firms working on Britney's case. The anonymous caller broke confidentiality with allegations that Britney was institutionalized in mid-January against her will. She hadn't started voluntary "me time" in April.

The caller alleged overhearing that co-conservator Andrew Wallet abruptly resigned due to worries about being disbarred. He failed to specify exactly how their 2019 plans were so much worse than what happened during the previous decade. Was it Britney's mistreatment, residency cancelation dealings, or some other scheme that was too unethical or outright illegal for him?

The caller also claimed that Jamie made the decision to blame the *Domination* cancelation on his own illness. The most chilling allegation was that long-time manager Larry Rudolph said sending Britney away would help with ticket revenue when they eventually re-announced the Las Vegas residency.

Podcast hosts Tess Barker and Barbara Gray gave the years-old #FreeBritney movement some mainstream media attention. Celebrity news sites jumped on the story.

One week later, Britney got to have Easter brunch with her boyfriend at the Montage hotel in Beverly Hills. Their exit was thoroughly photographed, despite her being picked up in an enclosed section of the luxury hotel's garage. Photos and video posted by the *Daily Mail* the next day showed her looking sedated and wearing messy hair, loose clothing, and slip-on sandals. (Wright, 2019)

Britney made an appearance in a closed hearing on her conservatorship at Stanley Mosk Courthouse on May 10. She reportedly told Judge Penny about her experiences during the previous four months in that facility. She recalled her reaction to the May 2019 hearing in her June 2021 statement:

> I haven't been back to court in a long time because I don't think I was heard on any level when I came to court the last time. I brought four sheets of paper in my hands and wrote in length what I have been through the last four months before I came there. The people who did that to me should not be able to walk away so easily.
>
> The last time I spoke to you, by just keeping the conservatorship going and also keeping my dad in the loop made me feel like I was dead, like I didn't matter, like nothing had been done to me, like you thought I was lying or something. I'm telling you again. I'm not lying.

Later in the May 10 hearing, Judge Penny ordered a 730 report to inform her judgment about Britney's health and well-being. The report was due in September 2019. (Associated Press, 2019)

Chapter 14

Dissipate

The 730 report on the investigation of Britney Spears's welfare in early 2019 was due to Judge Brenda Penny in September. The month before, Britney's psychiatrist at the time, Dr. Timothy Benson, passed away. (Dillon, 2019) Britney said that he had abruptly taken her off her usual medication and prescribed lithium instead in her June 23, 2021 court statement. She also alleged that Dr. Benson "illegally, yes 100 per-cent abused me by the treatment he gave me." He was also identified as the person who advised that she should check in to the facility she had complained about in May 2019. Presumably, he would have been involved in an investigation of those incidents.

On August 24, 2019, the date of Dr. Benson's death, Jamie Spears was accused of child abuse against one of Britney's sons. Their father was granted a restraining order the next day to protect both the children and himself from Jamie. (Radar, 2019) Ultimately, no criminal charges were brought against him, but the restraining order remained in place. (Puente, 2019) He could no longer supervise Britney's time with her sons.

On September 9, 2019, Jamie petitioned Judge Penny to temporarily step down as the conservator of Britney's person due to his own illness. Judge Penny approved of Britney's care coordinator Jodi Montgomery temporarily becoming conservator of the person. This left Jamie with control over his daughter's estate.

On July 20, 2020, Jamie filed a Status Report regarding the conservatorship both under seal and fully redacted "except for the signature." When Britney's attorney Samuel Ingham objected to this, Judge Penny ordered Jamie to file an explanation justifying hiding the report's contents, due on August 19, 2020. Jamie and Mr. Ingham met in advance of that hearing, as Mr. Ingham reported,

> On August 7, 2020 an all day meet and confer was held with the aforementioned retired Superior Court judge [Aviva Bobb].
>
> Unfortunately, no agreement was reached on any issue.

As sole conservator of the estate, Jamie was required to submit the 2019 Twelfth Accounting for the estate in 2020. On August 6, 2020, he filed the report and on August 17, Mr. Ingham responded with his own report to Judge Penny. He reported that Britney preferred "a qualified corporate fiduciary" as conservator of her estate and wanted Jodi Montgomery to be the permanent conservator of her person.

At the August 19 hearing, Jamie surprised everyone with a petition to bring Andrew Wallet back as co-conservator of the estate. This led to Mr. Ingham's August 27 petition for a new conservator of the estate, Bessemer Trust Company of California, a qualified corporate fiduciary.

In between the back and forth petitions and oppositions about estate conservator, business management firm Tri Star Sports and Entertainment Group abruptly resigned. Jamie's attorney Geraldine Wyle reported Tri Star's resignation to Mr. Ingham in an email dated October 28, 2020, which he attached to his petition for the appointment of Bessemer:

> While Tri Star is assisting in transitioning the business management, Tri Star cannot wait to effectuate this

change until the process of putting Bessemer in place as co-conservator is complete, including getting Bessemer familiar enough with the assets, work to be done, and needs of the Estate sufficient so that the Co-Conservators can make decisions about what structure of the business management and administration of the estate is in Britney's best interests.

In order to avoid a complete disruption to the Estate and a gap in the provision of services, Jamie has retained, at least for now, Michael Kane of Miller Kaplan to step into Tri Star's place, effective November 1, and to serve as the business manager. Michael is aware that there will be a corporate fiduciary serving with Jamie, and there will inevitably be a restructuring of the allocation of duties and responsibilities between and among the Co-Conservators and Michael Kane's team, as well as the Miller Kaplan fee arrangement, potentially.

Although Mr. Ingham had accepted previous accounting reports without comment, expenses listed in the 2019 accounting raised some red flags. On November 10, 2020, Mr. Ingham filed explicit and detailed objections to the accounting report. These included overpayment to Tri Star, payment for personal legal fees of Tri Star owner Lou Taylor, back rent Jamie owed one of Britney's companies, and investment valuation discrepancies.

In response to the October 28 letter from Ms. Wyle, Mr. Ingham also filed concerns about Michael Kane—how he was chosen, how much he was being paid, and how much of the estate he had access to. By the end of the hearing, Bessemer was appointed conservator of the estate.

Unfortunately, Mr. Ingham repeatedly made technical and formatting errors in the proposed order that kept Judge Penny from signing it. It took him so long to submit an error-free order that by the time Judge Penny signed off on June 30, 2021, Bessemer no longer wanted the job. On July 2, 2021, they submitted their resignation to the Court.

Representatives for Bessemer maintained that to date they had "not been issued Letters of Conservatorship and [were] therefore not currently authorized to act, [had] taken no actions as Conservator, [had] made no decisions as Conservator, [had] received no assets of the Estate, [and had] taken no fees." Their rationale for resigning was simple:

> As a result of the Conservatee's testimony at the June 23 hearing, however, Petitioner has become aware that the Conservatee objects to the continuance of her Conservatorship and desires to terminate the Conservatorship. Petitioner has heard the Conservatee and respects her wishes.

Chapter 15

The Statement

Britney Spears had been silenced from publicly speaking about her conservatorship from the beginning. The strict control of conservator dad Jamie Spears cut off her unfiltered blog posts, voluntary interviews, and off-the-cuff comments.

Eventually, even her brief, innocuous Instagram posts went silent. Fans began to question, "Where is Britney?" In April 2019, the *Britney's Gram* podcast hosts Tess Barker and Barbara Gray received an answer from an anonymous caller. He made accusations about Britney being held in a mental health facility against her will.[1] (Barker & Gray, 2019)

After months of online tabloid coverage, and awareness efforts online and at rallies in front of Stanley Mosk Courthouse, mainstream media began to take the case seriously. *The Los Angeles Times* published a long-form explainer about the case on September 17, 2019. (Newberry, 2019) Other publications picked up the *Times* reporting, from *Us Magazine* to *Psychology Today*.

Throughout Britney's conservatorship, her conservators took efforts to keep the case out of the public eye as much as possible. They requested dozens of documents not only be redacted of private information, but fully sealed from public view.

---

[1] *See* Chapter 13: Break

When Jamie Spears submitted his surprise petition for Andrew Wallet to return as co-conservator of the estate on August 19, 2020, he also requested sealing that petition. One month later, on September 16, Britney's attorney Samuel Ingham responded with both a petition for Bessemer Trust Company of California to take on the estate conservatorship, and opposition to the motion to seal the new Andrew Wallet petition from the public. Mr. Ingham argued,

> With very few limited exceptions, California law provides presumptively for public access to judicial records and proceedings because the public has a legitimate interest in understanding how its court system operates. The California Constitution states broadly that "[t]he people have the right of access to information concerning the conduct of the people's business, and, therefore, the meetings of public officials and agencies shall be open to public scrutiny." Cal.Const., art. I, §3, subd. (b)(1).
>
> BRITNEY's conservatorship has attracted an unprecedented level of scrutiny from mainstream media and social media alike. Far from being a conspiracy theory or a "joke" as JAMES reportedly told the media, in large part this scrutiny is a reasonable and even predictable result of JAMES' aggressive use of the sealing procedure over the years to minimize the amount of meaningful information made available to the public. Whatever merits his strategy might have had years ago when BRITNEY was trying to restart her career, at this point in her life when she is trying to regain some measure of personal autonomy, BRITNEY welcomes and

appreciates the informed support of her many fans. Although the sealing motion is supposedly for her "protection", BRITNEY herself is vehemently opposed to this effort by her father to keep her legal struggle hidden away in the closet as a family secret.

The moment that JAMES obtained from this Court the power to handle BRITNEY'S affairs on her behalf, he surrendered a large measure of privacy as to the manner in which he exercises that power. Transparency is an essential component in order for this Court to earn and retain the public's confidence with respect to protective proceedings like this one. In this case, it is not an exaggeration to say that the whole world is watching.

#FreeBritney became a rallying cry and pop culture curiosity until the release of *The New York Times Presents* documentary "Framing Britney Spears" on February 5, 2021. (Day & Stark, 2021a) The program kicked up sympathy for Britney and drew attention to little-known probate conservatorships. Four months later, Judge Brenda Penny's courtroom was finally open to the public to hear directly from Britney about her 13-year long case.

On June 22, 2021, the day before the hearing, the journalists behind "Framing Britney Spears" published the article, "Britney Spears Quietly Pushed for Years to End Her Conservatorship". (Day, Stark, & Coscarelli, 2021) They referenced confidential documents such as welfare evaluation reports, financial agreements, and a sealed hearing transcript. The article painted a picture of abuse and calls for help papered over by the machinery of probate courts that were set up for managing estates and not live people.

When the big day came, Britney called into the hearing remotely via L.A. Court Connect due to Covid-related restrictions. She spoke for over twenty minutes. Her statement was recorded online, so the whole world had the opportunity to hear her words in her own voice. A key subject of Britney's statement on June 23, 2021 was reporting the abuse she experienced in early 2019. She had spoken to Judge Brenda Penny about it right afterwards, but did not feel that anything had improved:[2]

> I'm telling you this again two years later, after I've lied and told the whole world I'm okay and I'm happy. It's a lie. I thought I—just maybe if I said that enough maybe I might become happy, because I've been in denial. I've been in shock. I am traumatized. You know, *fake it till you make it.* But now I'm telling you the truth, okay? I'm not happy. I can't sleep. I'm so angry it's insane. And I'm depressed. I cry every day. And the reason I'm telling you this is because I don't think how the state of California can have all this written in the court documents from the time I showed up, and do absolutely nothing. Just hire, with my money, another person to keep my dad on-board.
>
> Ma'am, my dad and anyone involved in this conservatorship, and my management who played a huge role in punishing me when I said *No,* ma'am, they should be in jail.
>
> I want changes, and I want changes going forward. I deserve changes.

---

[2] *See* Chapter 13: Break

I didn't want to say it openly because I honestly don't think anyone would believe me. To be honest with you, the Paris Hilton story [*I Am Paris*] on what they did to her at that school, I didn't believe any of it. I'm sorry. And I'm an outsider and I'll just be honest. I didn't believe it. And maybe I'm wrong, and that's why I didn't want to say any of this to anybody, to the public, because people would make fun or me or laugh at me and say, "She's lying. She's got everything. She's Britney Spears."

I'm not lying. I just want my life back. And it's been 13 years and it's enough. It's been a long time since I've owned my money. And it's my wish and my dream for all of this to end without being tested. Again, it makes no sense whatsoever for the state of California to sit back and literally watch me with their own two eyes, make a living for so many people and pay so many people trucks and buses on tour, on the road with me, and be told I'm not good enough. But I'm great at what I do. And I allow these people to control what I do, ma'am, and it's enough. It makes no sense at all.

The whole conservatorship from the beginning, once you see someone, whoever it is in the conservatorship making money, making their money and myself money and working, that whole statement right there, the conservatorship should end. I shouldn't be in a conservatorship if I can work and provide money and work for myself and pay other people. It makes no sense. The laws need to change. What state allows people to own another person's money and account and threaten them in saying, "You can't spend your money unless you do what we want you to do." And I'm paying them.

Ma'am, I've worked since I was 17 years old. You have to understand how thin that is for me every morning I get up to know I can't go somewhere unless I meet people I don't know every week in an office identical to the one where the therapist was very abusive to me. I truly believe this conservatorship is abusive, and that we can sit here all day and say, "Oh, conservatorships are here to help people." But, ma'am, there's a thousand conservatorships that are abusive as well.

I also would like to be able to share my story with the world and what they did to me instead of it being a hush-hush secret to benefit all of them. I want to be able to be heard on what they did to me by making me keep this in for so long. It's not good for my heart.

I have the right to use my voice and take up for myself. My attorney says I can't, it's not good. I can't let the public know anything they did to me. And by not saying anything is saying it's okay.

I know my lawyer, Sam [Ingham], has been very scared for me to go forward because he's saying if I speak up I'm being overworked in that facility, that rehab place, the rehab place will sue me. He told me I should keep it to myself, really. I would personally like to—actually, I know I have grown with a personal relationship with

Sam, my lawyer. I've been talking to him, like, three times a week now. We've kind of built a relationship, but I haven't really had the opportunity by my own self to actually handpick my own lawyer by myself, and I would like to be able to do that.

I want to end the conservatorship without having to be evaluated. I've done a lot of research, ma'am, and there's a lot of judges who do end conservatorships for people without them having to be evaluated all the time. The only times they don't is if a concerned family member says something's wrong with this person, and consider it otherwise, and considering my family has lived off my conservatorship for 13 years, I won't be surprised if one of them has something to say and go forward and say, "We don't think this should end. We have to help her." Especially if I get my fair turn in exposing what they did to me.

I'm honestly new with this, and I'm doing research on all of these things. I do know common sense and the method that things can end. For people it has ended without them being evaluated. So I just want you to take that in consideration.

I would like to progressively move forward, and I want to have the real deal. I want to be able to get married and have a baby. I was told right now in the conservatorship I'm not able to get married or have a baby. I have an [I.U.D.] inside of myself right now so I don't get pregnant. I wanted to take the [I.U.D.] out so I could start trying to have another baby, but this so-called team won't let me go to the doctor to take it out because they don't want me to have children, any more children. So basically this conservatorship is doing me way more harm than good.

I deserve to have a life. I've worked my whole life. I deserve to have a two- to three-year break and just, you know, do what I want to do. But I do feel like there is a crutch here, and I feel like I feel open and I'm okay to talk to you today about it, but I wish I could stay with you on the phone forever because when I get off the phone with you, all of a sudden, all I hear—all of these *no's. No. No. No.* And then all of a sudden, I get—I feel ganged up on, and I feel bullied, and I feel left out and alone. And I'm tired of feeling alone. I deserve to have the same rights as anybody does by having a child, a family, any of those things, and more so.

Chapter 16

Freed

Once the world heard about Britney Spears's experiences in her own words on June 23, 2021, movement on her case kicked into gear. On July 6, she was finally allowed to hire an attorney of her choice, Mathew Rosengart. On July 14, 2021, she made a second statement to Judge Brenda Penny, albeit in a closed courtroom:

> I also, again, want to petition the Court to end the conservatorship, but only if I don't have to be evaluated. I'm not sure why my lawyer [Samuel Ingham] didn't have an answer for me on that—my previous lawyer, not this lawyer now [Mathew Rosengart]. I also know that by law you can eliminate the evaluation if you choose. In some states that is permitted. I just want you to understand how much of my time it has taken by forcing me to do these stupid psych tests and nothing comes out of it.
>
> I know you're probably wondering why I wouldn't just get it over with and be evaluated. Well, it's because when I even did—before I was sent to that place, I had done three other psych tests that were against my will while I was working through *Circus* and all my tours. They said, "If you do well, we'll end it." I did these tests and had to go to that building in Beverly Hills two hours

at a time and I did those while working in the middle of a tour like four or five years, and they did nothing.

They did nothing under the conservatorship. They didn't end it. I just kept working. It was just a way to keep me working, so I'm not willing to take the chance and petition the conservatorship to end it for people to sit me down and question my intelligence for the millionth time. I have too much pride. So, yes, I would rather Jodi [Montgomery] stay in place at this point with me, with my future goals to make different rules that benefit me.

I'm here to get rid of my dad and charge him for conservatorship abuse. And frankly, I'm not really sure how immediate restraining orders placed on my dad after breaking a huge door down to get to my son and shaking him, and we all have to think and wonder if my dad is abusive to me.

I want to press charges for abuse on behalf of this conservatorship today, all of it, and removing my conservator. Instead of him trying to investigate my situation or my capacity or observing my behavior for the past 13 years, I want an investigation on my dad.

On July 26, 2021, twenty days after joining the case, Mr. Rosengart filed a petition to suspend Jamie Spears as conservator of Britney's estate. Over the next two months, the teams of attorneys of Britney and Jamie fired off volleys of petitions and supplements and oppositions about removing Jamie from the conservatorship.

For example, on August 12, Jamie's attorney Vivian Thoreen responded to the petition to suspend him with several pages about mom Lynne Spears's supporting declaration—not the actual petition. The response not only included personal attacks on her but also disingenuous claims that he was not the conservator of Britney's person while she was institutionalized against her will in 2019.

On Britney's side, Mr. Rosengart filed a last-minute supplement to their initial petition to remove Jamie on September 24. The supplement called for an investigation of allegations reported in *The New York Times* that the security firm hired to keep tabs on Britney used a recording device in her bedroom without her knowledge. (Day & Stark, 2021b)

On September 29, Judge Penny determined, "The pleadings appear to the Court to reflect a toxic environment which requires suspension of James Spears, as conservator of the estate of Britney Spears, effective today. This change, the Court finds, is in the best interest of the conservatee, which is my focus."

After Judge Penny made her order, Ms. Thoreen began discussing whether the suspension could be appealed. Unfortunately for Jamie, Judge Penny denied that possibility: "Under the code section I went under, it's not an appealable order, 2654."

In Britney's court statement in June 2021, she told Judge Penny, "I didn't know that I could petition the conservatorship to end it. I'm sorry for my ignorance, but I honestly didn't know that."

The first thing Judge Penny did after Britney finished talking was address her court-appointed lawyer, saying, "So, you know, Mr. Ingham, you know that there are methods to get conservatorships terminated. And if that's something that you're looking at doing, you know you can certainly file a petition for the Court to consider that." He never did file a petition to end the conservatorship.

On September 7, 2021, Jamie petitioned to end the conservatorship as one response to the petition to remove him from the case. On September 22, Britney filed her consent to terminate the conservatorships of her estate and person. However, Mr. Rosengart held off on actively joining the petition until October 1, after Jamie was removed from the case on September 29. In the October joinder, Mr. Rosengart stated that, "the suspended Conservator of the Estate (Mr. Spears), the Temporary Conservator of the Estate, and the Conservator of the Person Jodi Montgomery all consent to termination of the conservatorship on November 12, 2021."

When November 12 arrived, Judge Penny ultimately ordered the termination of the conservatorship thusly,

> In this case, the Court finds that this was a voluntary conservatorship, that there was no capacity declaration filed stating that Britney Spears lacked capacity, and therefore, there is no need for a submission by her of a capacity declaration stating that she has capacity for the Court to consider in making an order terminating the conservatorship.
>
> Further, all parties agree to the termination. The Court has read and considered the petition to terminate the conservatorship filed by James Spears, although now suspended, he was then serving as conservator of the estate at the time the petition was filed.
>
> Mr. Spears has since filed a status report and supplement to his petition stating his full agreement with the termination of the conservatorship without reservation

or condition.

The Court has read and considered the joinder and agreement to the termination of the conservatorship filed by the conservatee, Britney Jean Spears, as well as the consent filed by temporary conservator of the person of Britney Jean Spears, Jodi [Pais] Montgomery, and the consent of Lynne Spears, the conservatee's mother.

Based on the foregoing, the Court finds and determines that a conservatorship of the person and estate of Britney Jean Spears is no longer required.

Chapter 17

Accounting

Judge Brenda Penny's November 12, 2021 order to terminate Britney Spears's conservatorship included a caveat:

> John Zabel, as a follow-up and conclusion of his services as temporary conservator of the estate is to file a substituted judgment, which shall be assigned a hearing date of December 8, 2021 at 1:30 PM in this department. John Zabel is also ordered to transfer assets into the trust.

During that December 8 hearing, Judge Penny finally ordered, "Britney Jean Spears has the ability to execute documents in transacting business on her own behalf and that any previous order entered by this court regarding restricting her ability to sign estate plan documents is revoked."

Although the conservatorship had been terminated, the case continued in probate court. The accounting report for 2019 had a few charges that still needed investigating. This included a payment of $308,974 to Tri Star Sports and Entertainment Group beyond their contracted amount. In attorney Samuel Ingham's November 6, 2020 objections to the accounting, he presented an exchange between Tri Star executives and then-conservator Jamie Spears as evidence that they did less work than in previous years, but were paid more:

On Nov 12, 2019, at 10:50 AM, Lou Taylor wrote:

Jamie -

We just ran time and billing for Britney and all of the entities. We have a (400k) loss on time and billing this year - we have been paid &179k.

I want to stay at 5 percent commission but set a floor of $500k a year.

Meaning we would not get paid less than the $500k this year & 2020 so we would get a retainer payment each month and each quarter settle it up against the commission. Unlike the other professionals management and legal we are still having to do work even though B is not including the court accounting.

Then next year we will look at time and billing again.

Is this approved?

Coram Deo,

Lou Taylor

On Nov 12, 2019, at 6:42 PM, Jamie Spears

Sorry my head trying to get all this going on straight will get back to you

Sent from my iPhone

From: Lou Taylor
Sent: Tuesday, November 12, 2019 6:57 PM
To: Jamie Spears
Cc: Robin Greenhill

Subject: Re: Retainer against commission Tri Star

Yes I know Robin and I were supposed to go through it with you- know it's bad timing. We just want to create a floor since we can't afford to lose 400k. We are looking to true up 2019

Meaning the floor is we won't make less than the 500k a year and if commission is at least that we will true it up.

Coram Deo,
Lou Taylor

On Dec 20, 2019, at 11:29 AM, Robin Greenhill wrote:
Here is the calculation based on the below.
[REDACTED]

Robin Greenhill
[REDACTED]

From: Jamie Spears
Sent: Friday, December 20, 2019 1:10 PM
To: Robin Greenhill
Subject:Re: Retainer against commission Tri Star

Approved

Sent from my iPhone

There was also a separate additional payment of $80,000 to Tri Star beyond their contracted amount. Ms. Taylor's legal fees of over $350,000 for a personal lawsuit were billed to Britney's estate. Jamie owed back rent on space owned by Britney's company Bridgemore Timber. And $77,725 for "Investment Valuation Differences" needed a full explanation.

On March 26, 2021, a new petition for payments to Jamie's attorneys was filed with Los Angeles Superior Court. However, mom Lynne Spears objected to these fees billed by Vivian Thoreen, another attorney who helped start the conservatorship in 2008. Ms. Thoreen's firm, Holland & Knight (H&K), had been hired to represent Jamie in litigation regarding the 2019 conservatorship accounting. However, their $893,751 bill for four months of work included approximately $220,000 for "media matters" that Lynne considered inappropriate. If you saw Ms. Thoreen on a TV show or in a documentary between 2020-2021, that's what Britney was billed for.

Lynne's March 26, 2021 objections to the fee and cost request from Holland & Knight stated,

> Petitioner submits that the fees requested by H&K are substantively improper in that the services were unrelated to the Purpose outlined by Mr. Spears for retaining H&K, outside of H&K's experience as touted in the Petition, unnecessary, and not performed in good faith for the benefit of the Conservatee, but instead largely constituted a "national media tour" orchestrated by H&K to promote Ms. Thoreen and/or to combat media cover-age that cast Mr. Spears in a negative light.
>
> Over and above the hours logged for the approved Purpose, within the disclosed experience, for the approved attorneys, however, are 385.1 hours at rates ranging from $360/hr. to $900/hr. plus "non-H&K litigation communication and media response consultants, whose hourly billing rates range from $35/hr. to $650/hr." logged by "H&K's litigation communication and global media response team for the benefit and

protection of the estate."

Petitioner submits that all of the time and expense related to this national media tour is not at all "necessary and performed in good faith for the benefit of the Conservatee," and in fact, is directly contrary to her wish for privacy. The Conservatee's life has been under a media microscope, and the last thing she wishes, desires, or derives any benefit from is her Conservator's attorney spending Conservatee's money to promote herself in the same media that scrutinizes everything that happens to the Conservatee.

In Jamie's August 12, 2021 response to the petition to remove him from the conservatorship, he denied that there was any reason why removal was necessary less than two months after Britney's public accusations of his abuse. He agreed that he should eventually step down from the role, but only after pending matters such as accounting were resolved:

Mr. Spears hopes to work with the Court and Ms. Spears' new attorney to resolve pending matters related to his acts as Conservator, such as the pending Twelfth Account and a final account, to facilitate a smooth transition. When these matters are resolved, Mr. Spears will be in a position to step aside.

As of October 2023, the accounting from the last couple years of the conservatorship still hadn't been settled.

Throughout the conservatorship, Britney was billed many millions of dollars by attorneys representing her and her conservators in conservatorship proceedings. Court-appointed lawyer Mr. Ingham's annual fees topped $400,000 by the time he resigned in July 2021. His replacement brought a team of attorneys to the case. Mathew Rosengart was joined by five other attorneys from the firm of Greenberg & Traurig. Britney had more people in her corner and paid for the privilege.

Even people who didn't work for her or the conservatorship expected her to cover their legal bills. Despite the fact that she was under no obligation to do so, people still petitioned Judge Penny to force Britney to pay.

When Britney's mom stepped in as an interested party to the conservatorship, she was represented by legal teams in both her home state of Louisiana and in California. The four attorneys gave her a 40% discount, setting the bill at $663,202.

After her dad was removed from his position as conservator, the attorneys who had been with him since starting the conservatorship resigned. Any debts he incurred outside of his role as conservator had to be paid out of his own pocket. That didn't stop his new lawyer from petitioning for payment from his daughter.

Although the conservatorships ended in November 2021, as of October 2023, there continued to be volleys of deposition requests and subpoenas for evidence and oppositions against and motions for them between Britney's new attorneys and those representing the former conservatorship team. Mr. Rosengart wanted Jamie to explain his financial dealings and possible conflicts of interest. Jamie wanted to question a whistleblower on the record to counter allegations of abuse. Mr. Rosengart wanted Jamie's former lawyers and business managers to justify their billing. Jamie wanted to grill Britney about her accusations of abuse. And she continued paying for her freedom.

Works Cited

The Associated Press. (2019, May 10). The Latest: Spears, parents talk in court; evaluation sought. *AP News.* www.apnews.com/article/ 86d57dc8c80e46d5bcc390f83bb856d6

Bailey, F. & Barbato, R. (Directors). (2013). *I Am Britney Jean* [Film]. World of Wonder Productions.

Barker, T. & Gray, B. (Hosts). (2019, April 16). #FREE BRITNEY (No. 75) [Audio podcast episode]. In *Britney's Gram.* britneysinstagram.libsyn.com/75-freebritney

Billboard Staff. (2018, July 20). Billboard's 2018 Money Makers: 50 Highest-Paid Musicians. *Billboard.* www.billboard.com/ photos/billboards-2018-money-makers-50-highest-paid-musicians/

Blankstein, A., Gold, S., & Winton, R. (2008, January 31). Precision teamwork in Spears operation. *The Los Angeles Times.* www.latimes.com/news/la-me-britney31jan31-story.html

Britney: Live in Concert. (Accessed 2023, September 30). In *Wikipedia.* en.wikipedia.org/w/index.php?title=Britney: _Live_in_Concert&oldid=1177321372

Britney: Piece of Me. (Accessed 2023, September 30). In *Wikipedia.* en.wikipedia.org/w/index.php?title=Britney: _Piece_of_Me&oldid=1168563114

Brooks, D. (2019, January 4). Britney Spears' Domination Las Vegas Residency Cancellation Could Cost Her Millions. *Billboard.* www.billboard.com/pro/britney-spears-domination-las-vegas-residency-cancellation-cost-millions/

California Courts. (Accessed 2023, September 20). *Adult Civil Mental Health.* www.courts.ca.gov/48654.htm

Carr, E.L. (Director). (2021). *Britney vs. Spears* [Film]. Carr Lot Productions & Story Syndicate. www.netflix.com

Craker, L. & Spears, L. (2008). *Through The Storm: A Real Story of Fame and Family in a Tabloid World.* Thomas Nelson Publishing.

Day, L. (Writer). & Stark, S. (Director). (2021, February 5). Framing Britney Spears (Season 1, Episode 6) [TV series episode]. In Robertson, M. (Executive Producer), *The New York Times Presents.* Left/Right & Seven.One Studios.

Day, L., Stark, S., & Coscarelli, J. (2021, June 22). Britney Spears Quietly Pushed for Years to End Her Conservatorship. *The New York Times.* www.nytimes.com/2021/06/22/arts/music/britney-spears-conservatorship.html

Day. L. & Stark, S. (2021, September 24). The Surveillance Apparatus That Surrounded Britney Spears. *The New York Times.* www.nytimes.com/2021/09/24/arts/music/ britney-spears-conservatorship-documentary.html

Dean, A. (Director & Writer). (2020). *I Am Paris* [Film]. The Intellectual Property Corporation.

Dennis, A. (2008, October 6). Lynne Spears: 'Things Are Looking Up Again'. *People.* www.people.com/celebrity/lynne-spears-things-are-looking-up-again/

Dillon, N. (2019, September 9). Britney Spears' doc dies of reported aneurysm just weeks before judge takes up report on her medical treatment and conservatorship. *The New York Daily News.* www.nydailynews.com/2019/09/09/britney-spears-doc-dies-of-reported-aneurysm-just-weeks-before-judge-takes-up-report-on-her-medical-treatment-and-conservatorship/

Farrow, R. & Tolentino, J. (2021, July 3). Britney Spears's Conservatorship Nightmare. *The New Yorker.* www.newyorker.com/news/american-chronicles/britney-spears-conservatorship-nightmare

Femme Fatale Tour. (Accessed 2023, October 2). In *Wikipedia.* en.wikipedia.org/w/index.php?title= Femme_Fatale_Tour &oldid=1176812560

Götting, M.C. (2023, August 29). Recorded music market revenue worldwide 2005-2022. *Statista.* www.statista.com/statistics/292081/music-revenue-worldwide-by-source/

Griffin, P. (2008). *Britney: For the Record* [Film]. RadicalMedia.

James Spears. (Accessed 2023, September 20). in *Corporation Wiki.* www.corporationwiki.com/Tennessee/Brentwood/james-p-spears/

Kovaleski, S.F. & Coscarelli, J. (2016, May 4). Is Britney Spears Ready to Stand on Her Own? *The New York Times.* www.nytimes.com/2016/05/08/arts/music/is-britney-spears-ready-to-stand-on-her-own.html

Legaspi, A. (2018, October 18). Britney Spears Announces New Las Vegas 'Domination' Residency. *Rolling Stone.* www.rollingstone.com/music/music-news/britney-spears-new-las-vegas-residency-domination-park-mgm-744595/

McGee, T. (2008, February 1). Britney Treated By 'Caring, Concerned' Therapist. *People.* www.people.com/celebrity/britney-treated-by-caring-concerned-therapist/

Newberry, L. (2019, September 18). Britney Spears hasn't fully controlled her life for years. Fans insist it's time to #FreeBritney. *The Los Angeles Times.* www.latimes.com/california/story/2019-09-17/britney-spears-conservatorship-free-britney

Piece of Me Tour. (Accessed 2023, September 30). *Wikipedia.*

en.wikipedia.org/w/index.php?title=Piece_of_Me_Tour&oldid=1172174642

Puente, M. (2019, September 18). Britney Spears' father won't be charged with child abuse, prosecutor says. *USA Today.* www.usatoday.com/story/entertainment/celebrities/2019/09/18/britney-spears-dad-jamie-wont-charged-child-abuse-prosecutor-says/2362531001/

Radar Staff. (2019, September 3). Britney Spears' Father Jamie Investigated For Alleged Abuse Of Singer's Son. *Radar Online.* www.radaronline.com/exclusives/2019/09/britney-spears-father-jamie-alleged-abuse-kevin-federline-son-police-report/

Superior Court of Calif., Cty of San Diego. (2019). *General Conservatorship of the Person Packet PKT-045.* www.sdcourt.ca.gov/sdcourt/probate2/probateforms

Vacco-Bolanos, J. (2019, January 7). Britney Spears and Her Boyfriend Sam Asghari Grab In-N-Out Burger After She Puts Vegas Shows on Hold: Pics. *Us Weekly.* www.usmagazine.com/celebrity-news/pictures/britney-spears-sam-asghari-grab-in-n-out-burger-photos/

Wright, T. (2019, April 22). Britney Spears seen for the first time on Easter Sunday... weeks after checking into mental health facility following her father's health concerns. *Daily Mail.* www.dailymail.co.uk/tvshowbiz/article-6947331/ Britney-Spears-seen-time-Easter-weeks-checking-mental-health-facility.html

About the Author

R. J. Ilyn studied Digital Arts at the University of California, which helped in designing and running FreeBritney.net. A native of California, Ilyn resides in the Bay Area with family and redwood trees. "Heaven On Earth" is her very favorite Britney Spears song.

Acknowledgements

Thank you to The DōsMan for all of your support and affection.

Thank you to Sara for asking all the right questions.

Thank you to all the people who make the internet happen and to all the researchers who came before me.

Made in the USA
Middletown, DE
28 May 2024